CONFLICT AND ITS RESOLUTION IN CONTEMPORARY AFRICA

Edited by
Harry G. West

Series Editor
Kenneth W. Thompson

Volume IX
In the Miller Center Series on
A World in Change

UNIVERSITY PRESS OF AMERICA
Lanham • New York • Oxford

The Miller Center
University of Virginia

University Press of America,® Inc.
4720 Boston Way
Lanham, Maryland 20706

12 Hid's Copse Rd.
Cummor Hill, Oxford OX2 9JJ

Printed in the United States of America
British Cataloging in Publication Information Available

Copublished by arrangement with The Miller Center of Public Affairs,
University of Virginia

The views expressed by the author(s) of this publication do not necessarily represent the opinions of the Miller Center. We hold to Jefferson's dictum that: "Truth is the proper and sufficient antagonist to error, and has nothing to fear from the conflict, unless by human interposition, disarmed of her natural weapons, free argument and debate."

Library of Congress Cataloging-in-Publication Data

Conflict and its resolution in contemporary Africa / edited by Harry G. West ; series editor, Kenneth W. Thompson.
p. cm. -- (Miller Center series on a world in change ; v. 9)
1. Africa, Sub-Saharan--Politics and government--1960--Congresses. 2. Africa, Sub-Saharan--Foreign relations--1960--Congresses. 3. Intervention (International law)--Congresses. 4. International police--Congresses. I. West, Harry G. II. Thompson, Kenneth W. III. Series.
DT352.8.C64 1997 967.03'2--dc21 97-22393 CIP

ISBN: 978-0-7618-0851-0

∞™ The paper used in this publication meets the minimum requirements of American National Standard for Information Sciences—Permanence of Paper for Printed Library Materials, ANSI Z39.48–1984.

To
Harry West
and his generation
who have taken up the torch

Kenneth W. Thompson
Series Editor

Contents

PREFACE ... vii
Kenneth W. Thompson

INTRODUCTION ... ix
Harry G. West

1. ETHNIC CONFLICT IN AFRICA: A JOURNALIST'S VIEW ... 1
Bill Berkeley

2. COLLAPSED STATES IN AFRICA ... 19
I. William Zartman

3. ETHIOPIA: YESTERDAY AND TODAY ... 39
John W. Harbeson

4. THE UNITED STATES, THE UNITED NATIONS, AND SOMALIA ... 55
Admiral Jonathan T. Howe

5. PEACEKEEPING AND HUMANITARIAN CRISES ... 73
Robert B. Oakley

6. SOMALIA: REFLECTIONS ON U.S. INTERVENTION ... 93
Stevenson McIlvaine

7. LIMITATIONS TO UNITED NATIONS PEACEMAKING IN AFRICA ... 109
Thomas P. Sheehy

8. GENOCIDE IN RWANDA AND THE INTERNATIONAL RESPONSE ... 123
Alison L. Des Forges

Preface

KENNETH W. THOMPSON

One of the rewards of teaching is Harry West. If that cryptic statement needs explanation, I would reminisce that West was an undergraduate student who studied international relations with me at the University of Virginia. He also was a writer and editor at the Miller Center along with other activities that reflected his commitment to society and his interests. One such activity was his work at the University of Virginia Medical Center and his involvement in drug rehabilitation. No effort was too demanding nor too stressful. He followed a canon of responsibility that reflected his family values and his inner sense of what most needed doing.

We were saddened when he left the University of Virginia for graduate studies in anthropology at the University of Wisconsin in Madison. Soon we learned that he was a standout in that program as he pursued his doctorate. He won several awards, one of which was a highly competitive national fellowship in which he was at the top of the list of recipients.

Through his years at Wisconsin, Harry remained in touch with some of us at U.Va., actually doing the final phase of the writing of his dissertation in Charlottesville. Over several years, we had invited leading Africanists to conduct forums, and West joined in some of the discussions, being responsible for forums in the last stage of the project.

With his authoritative knowledge of African studies, countries, and personalities, it was natural that we should invite him to organize and edit the volume. The rest is history, as they say. The volume is a product of his knowledge and imagination. He has taken up the torch of responsibility at the Miller Center, and we all are the beneficiaries. We salute him at the start of a bright and very promising career. He is certain to be a leader in anthropology.

Introduction

HARRY G. WEST

Despite the dawn of the "New World Order," recent years have brought conflict and chaos to some African nations. What little American audiences have seen of Africa has provided them with images of violence–rebel forces under an opposition commander torturing, mutilating, and finally executing the captured president of Liberia; Somali militiamen dragging the body of an American soldier through the streets of Mogadishu; dismembered Rwandans piled in and around the churches and hospitals where they sought refuge from genocidal fury. To the extent that bloody scenes such as these challenge the notion of a New World Order, Africa has been made grounds for testing the dynamics of that Order in crisis, as well as for determining the meaning of that Order for citizens of the New World. In this decade, the United Nations has deployed or mandated peacekeeping or peacemaking forces throughout the African continent, including substantial operations in Namibia, Angola, Somalia, Mozambique, and Rwanda.

Humanitarian concerns necessitate an analysis of the effectiveness of these interventions as means for the preclusion of human tragedy. In crasser terms, policy practitioners also consider the interests at stake to their own nations and weigh the relative costs–however defined–of involvement or noninvolvement. In any case, to better understand the disorder witnessed today in selected African nations, one must examine both the complex historical contexts that have given rise to African nation-states and the contemporary conflicts within them, and the ways in which recent dramatic changes in global political structures have framed these conflicts. The chapters in this volume–each drawn from a presentation made at the White Burkett Miller Center at the University of Virginia in Charlottesville between July 1993 and May 1995—contribute to this task.

The first two chapters outline broad theoretical issues. In chapter one, free-lance journalist Bill Berkeley places contemporary African conflicts in perspective, reminding us that war and genocide are neither exclusively or quintessentially African phenomena. He asks, "What is it that brings out this reaction in people? and . . . why is it happening now?" Berkeley questions the thesis that the ethnic dimensions of conflict can be attributed simply to the arbitrary borders laid down by colonial powers, pointing out that inter-ethnic strife is an exceptional event in Africa rather than the norm. Instead, Berkeley traces the roots of conflict to the authoritarian and corrupt exercise of power over the state.

As a vivid example of corruption, Berkeley details the involvement of former Rwandan president Juvénal Habyarimana in illicit activities ranging from marijuana smuggling to trafficking in mountain guerrillas to black marketeering in hard currencies. Many of Africa's corrupt "big men," he adds, are also military men whose careers can be traced to their roles as "collaborators" with colonial powers prior to independence, and later as proxies in the Cold War. To protect their personal interests, Berkeley tells us, these "tyrants" play the card of ethnicity to divide and weaken potential opposition. In countries with high levels of illiteracy, their monopoly over state media such as radio allows them to orchestrate and manipulate social tensions that sometimes erupt into civil war.

In chapter two, I. William Zartman, professor of international organization and conflict resolution, also warns against viewing all of Africa through the lens of chaos, asserting that "much in Africa is quiet, stable, and still functioning." Although there is nothing about African society that makes the state an inappropriate political institution, he argues, specific African nations have suffered from a phenomenon he calls the "collapsed state." A collapsed state, he tells us, is distinctive from one challenged by rebellion, coup, or even revolution; it is a state where the very notion of legitimate authority is challenged, and law and order break down.

Zartman identifies waves of state collapse in postindependence African history, the first wave striking nations such as Uganda, Chad, and Mauritania in the 1970s and the next beginning in the

1980s and culminating in places such as Liberia, Somalia, and Rwanda. In the typical case, he suggests, collapse has come after a regime has concentrated power to the point where it provokes near universal opposition from the society it unconvincingly claims to represent. Under siege, the regime itself may then splinter, and none of those competing for power are able to consolidate their position with sufficient support. A vacuum emerges at the center of power, and the state ceases to function. While Zartman does not claim to offer prescriptions for the reconstitution of the state, he does suggest that attempts to reestablish order must be linked with efforts to exercise once more the functions of the state. To achieve this, he warns, compromises must be made and contradictions overcome: An emerging governing coalition must attain legitimacy despite its rise in the context of foreign intervention, deals between suspect but powerful individuals and political groups (including many responsible for state collapse in the first place), and probable postponement of genuine democratic processes.

The third chapter provides a historical perspective on one state struggling against collapse: Ethiopia. John Harbeson, professor of political science, points out that although Ethiopia is the only African nation to have avoided colonial conquest, it has periodically struggled to maintain internal cohesion since the middle the 19th century. The individual statesmanship of Emperor Haile Selassie—who co-opted elites from within various regions and ethnic groups—consolidated the empire after World War II, but at the cost of undermining potential successors. The military committee that overthrew Selassie in 1974 saw in his clients political threats, he explains, and moved to eliminate their power through revolutionary policies, including significant land reform. In its pursuit of revolution, however, the regime of Mengistu Haile-Mariam lost contact with its popular base of support and encountered mounting resistance from regionally based ethnic movements in Eritrea, Tigre, and elsewhere. Eventually, Mengistu himself was overthrown by a Tigrean-led coalition of forces, which has looked to consolidate itself at the expense of other regionally based groups. As a result of these events, Harbeson wonders "whether there will be an Ethiopian State at all" in the future. Eritrean succession, he points out, represents the first successful challenge to the sanctity of independence-era borders, leading him to consider the possibility that "[w]hat happened to Eritrea may be replicated and we might see many states or statelets in that region."

In the next three chapters, Admiral Jonathan Howe (who served as United Nations' special representative for Somalia), Robert Oakley (former ambassador to Somalia), and Stevenson McIlvaine (who worked as deputy chief of mission of the U.S. Liaison Office in Mogadishu) reflect on their experiences in Somalia and the lessons of U.S. and U.N. involvement there. Howe's chapter briefly reviews the historical roots of conflict and state collapse in Somalia, as well as the chronology of foreign intervention. He states that the United States became militarily involved, with the approval of the United Nations, "because thousands of innocent people had been robbed of food relief shipments that had been sent in to feed them"; 300,000 had died, and another one-and-a-half million were expected to die in 1993. Nonetheless, leaders of the various Somali factions had not achieved any settlement, and for that reason, foreign intervention became an act of peace*making* and not peace*keeping*.

So long as intervention focused on attempts to "help the whole country recover"—including efforts to rebuild domestic political, economic, and security institutions, and to get schools, health facilities, water and electrical systems, and agriculture functioning once more—the operation moved ahead relatively successfully, Howe suggests. The viscous attack by Somali General Aideed on Pakistani troops soon after the transfer of mission leadership from the United States to the United Nations, however, brought about a dynamic that would increasingly distract the mission from its objectives; U.N. forces were drawn into taking sides in the conflict.

Robert Oakley discusses the significance of the Aideed attack and U.N. responses in greater detail in his chapter. When the United States originally committed troops to Somalia, it took precautions to ensure that it not be drawn into the conflict as it had been in Lebanon a decade earlier. As U.S. military officials passed responsibility on to U.N. commanders, they urged maintenance of close contacts with all Somali parties, even when relations with a particular party were tense. United Nations commanders were hesitant to follow this advice, however, and mistrust deepened between U.N. forces and Aideed. Once Aideed struck, the new Clinton administration was inclined to support a U.N. policy to identify "good" and "bad" Somalis and to eliminate "bad" ones as obstacles to the peace process. In attacking Aideed, the United Nations–and the United States–lost credibility among the Somali population and Aideed's portrayal of the operation as hostile foreign aggression gained credence. This turn of events produced the deaths of 18 U.S. servicemen–leading the American public and Somalis to question why U.S. troops were in Mogadishu.

In his chapter, Stevenson McIlvaine picks up on the issue of American public support for interventions like the one in Somalia. He suggests that when Americans witness large-scale suffering anywhere in the world–especially on television–they wish to see assistance provided. They are often unwilling to pay the cost, however, particularly if it means sending U.S. troops and accepting casualties. He casts the issue in stark terms: "The alternative to using military force when dealing with thugs is to say, 'This is not in our interest; it is not important to us; it is awful, but we are just going to turn our backs and let it happen.'" While McIlvaine himself does not espouse this position, he argues that U.S. citizens need to make hard choices about what they want their government to do and what they are willing to give to see it done.

Former Heritage Foundation Fellow Thomas Sheehy (more recently assistant to a congressman) addresses in his chapter a repeated question, namely, the viability of the United Nations as a vehicle for response. Reflecting on U.N. peacekeeping and peacemaking around the African continent as well as elsewhere in the world, he identifies the organization's inefficiencies, ineffectiveness, and ultimate lack of perceived neutrality. The United Nations, he suggests, always represents someone's interests but does a rather poor job of advancing those interests. Sheehy not only asserts that nations acting unilaterally could do a better job, but predicts that ". . . in the next five to ten years, people will realize that the United Nations has vastly overplayed its hand in terms of peacemaking operations. There will be a tendency for powers to act unilaterally." Observing that U.S. interests in Africa are limited in the post-Cold War era, however, Sheehy counsels restricted engagement there on the part of the United States.

Sheehy's discussion excludes what Howe refers to as "third tier problems" faced by the United States as a world leader. The third tier, in Howe's terms, includes genocide, ethnic cleansing, and starvation. Although the national interests of observer nations in these cases may be difficult to assess, involvement may be grounded on the transcendent plane of moral responsibility, Howe argues. Still, the Somalia scenario offers little incentive to place morality over interest, and only mixed evidence that such attempts will be rewarded with meaningful success. As Howe observes, "Somalia is . . . used as an excuse for inaction." Further complicating the matter is a desire exhibited by post-Cold War leaders to gain international consensus and cooperation for interventionary actions while at the same time preserving autonomy of action for troops placed in harm's way, as Howe notes. Oakley observes that this dilemma leads to postponement of action, which can be enormously costly in terms of wasted opportunities for the prevention or resolution of conflict and related human tragedies.

The final chapter provides a detailed rendering of this scenario. Alison Des Forges, human rights activist and professor of history, describes how reluctance to become involved in "another Somalia" prevented members of the international community from taking action in Rwanda, despite warnings and, later, undisputed accounts of massive and systematic violence. Her chapter begins with a succinct summary of the historical roots of conflict in Rwanda. Then, surveying many of the same issues raised by Berkeley and Zartman, she discusses how the Habyarimana regime–weakened by its growing isolation from Rwandan society–used ethnic tensions in its attempt to sure up its grasp on state power. When it was made clear to the regime that exiled former ruling elites from the minority Tutsi ethnic group–which had once collaborated with the colonial administration and treated the Hutu majority in Rwanda abusively–were about to cross the border into Rwanda with a guerrilla force, the regime did nothing to stop them. Instead, it waited until the guerrillas posed a credible threat and then incited Rwandan Hutus to respond by killing whatever Tutsi they could identify, including many Tutsi never exiled from Rwanda who represented a potentially legitimate opposition to the governing clique.

Despite the horrific images of slaughter coming out of Rwanda in the following weeks, both the United Nations and its constituent members remained paralyzed. In fact, a small U.N. contingent already in Rwanda was reduced to 270 soldiers after the brutal murder of 10 Belgian troops. The perpetrators of these murders, Des Forges asserts, knew that the cost of even ten lives was too high for the international community to accept as the price of intervention. Only after six more months of convulsive violence did the United Nations move back into Rwanda.

Des Forges does not pretend to have answers to the issues raised by other contributors to this volume, recognizing, for example, the futility of suggesting that U.S. troops be deployed in such a setting, where U.S. interests are not apparent. Still, she calls attention to the need for some form of concerted response on the part of the international community, which, she points out, ultimately pays dearly for such occurrences after the fact through humanitarian assistance to refugee communities. The bottom line, Des Forges asserts, is that "neutrality is not possible in the face of genocide." Hers is an argument difficult to ignore.

CHAPTER ONE

Ethnic Conflict in Africa: A Journalist's View*

BILL BERKELEY

NARRATOR: Recent discussions on violence, instability, and the collapse of states come together in the issue of ethnic conflict in Africa. Mr. Bill Berkeley is interested in these issues and whether or not what is happening in Africa also has previously occurred in other parts of the world.

Mr. Berkeley is a free-lance journalist and has written numerous articles in the *Atlantic Monthly* and *The New Republic*. He is a graduate of Harvard College and spent a year at Yale Law School on a fellowship for journalists. He spent three years as an investigative reporter on human rights violations in Africa and the Middle East. He is the author of two books on human rights and ethnic conflicts in Zimbabwe and Liberia, one which is entitled *Liberia: A Promise Betrayed* (1986).

Mr. Berkeley is uniquely qualified to demystify some of the notions concerning the uniqueness of Africa. He has worked in several African countries, recently including Uganda, Sudan, Ethiopia, Kenya, and post-election South Africa. Previously, he reported on Liberia, Zaire, Zimbabwe, Mozambique, and pre-election South Africa. He has just returned from east and southern Africa where, as the recipient of the distinguished Alicia Patterson Fellowship, he extensively explored the issue of genocide in

**Presented in a Forum at the Miller Center of Public Affairs on 8 May 1995.*

Rwanda. His approach is therefore a broad one, and we are delighted that he is speaking today.

MR. BERKELEY: As indicated, I have reported from a range of countries in east and southern Africa. I have made some generalizations about all of these countries and the considerable violence that has occurred in all of them, much of it having an ethnic dimension. I will attempt to identify the patterns that emerge in these different countries.

In Rwanda in 1994, approximately 500,000 people were murdered in about three months. In Liberia, the latest figures show that about 150,000 people have been killed. Sudan has been at war for 12 of the last 25 years (or about 30 of the last 40 years and 13 of the last 17 decades). According to the latest figures, about 1.3 million have died in the last decade in Sudan. In Kenya in 1982 and 1983—a country that receives less publicity—about 1,500 people were killed and approximately 300,000 more were rendered homeless in ethnic clashes in the Great Rift Valley. Beginning around 1992 in Zaire, 2,000 to 3,000 people have been killed and several hundred thousand made homeless in the southern province of Shaba. In South Africa the figures are small by African standards but alarming by any other standard. Between 15,000 and 20,000 people have been killed in violence in the townships and the southeast province of Natal. What I hope to do is tie these conflicts together, identify the common denominators, and address the question that probably has arisen in the minds of many people who have seen images of this horrific bloodshed on television. The question is, How can human beings be brought to a point where they are slaughtering each other in such enormous numbers? What is it that can possibly compel or coerce—as the case may be—people into slaughtering their fellow civilian populations?

First, it should be noted that these kinds of horrors are not unique to Africa. The widespread perception exists in this country—perhaps perpetuated by my colleagues in the press—that something is different and mysterious about Africa. When Hutus and Tutsis are shown slaughtering each other with machetes and clubs with nails sticking out of them, or when Xhosas and Zulus in the townships in South Africa are shown hacking each other to death, these images unfortunately feed a stereotype that there is some kind of inherent savagery that distinguishes Africans from the rest of humanity. I simply would like to remind people that these kinds of horrors have occurred in all parts of the world throughout all of history, not least in the middle of Europe in the middle of this century. The Holocaust is only the most obvious example, but by no means the only one. I have recently been pursuing confirmation of events like the rape of Nanking in China in 1937, when the Japanese slaughtered approximately 300,000 Chinese people in a matter of weeks. Not all of these conflicts have an ethnic base, but many do. Two million people were killed in the border between India and Pakistan in 1947 (at the time of the partition).

Ethnicity, however, is not always the issue. Stalin killed approximately 20 million people between 1931 and 1941. Stalin's police arrested about 19 million Soviet citizens and immediately shot around seven million outright. Another 20 million people in the former Soviet Union were starved to death in the great collectivization campaigns of the early 1930s. Harold Isaacs, the great scholar at MIT who wrote the seminal book on ethnicity and conflict in the 1970s, *Idols of the Tribe* (1975), estimated that about 10 million people were killed in approximately 34 major blood lettings involving group identity around the world between 1945 and 1974. The point is that although these kinds of huge scale massacres and killings in Africa are certainly evidence of the basest kind of savagery imaginable, they do not distinguish Africans from all of the peoples of the world throughout all of history. The relevant questions are first, What is it that brings out this reaction in people? and second, Why is it happening now?

The most common explanation for ethnic conflict in Africa is its arbitrary colonial borders. The colonial powers drew Africa's boundaries to suit their own colonial interests at the Berlin Conference in 1884. The boundaries had very little to do with Africa's diverse ethnic language groupings. They broke up some tribes while roping others together. This explanation assumes that Africa's tribes are inherently incapable of getting along with each other. It further assumes that there is something peculiar about tribes and something exotic or inscrutable about the cultural construct of these groupings that brings them into inevitable conflict. I have been reporting on and off from Africa for more than a decade, and that explanation does not work. Most of Africa's tribes get along with each other and live side by side in relative harmony.

Some vivid examples, such as Liberia, highlight the problem with this theory. Liberia has been at war since 1990. The principle protagonists in that war are two tribes: the Krahn and the Gio. The border on the eastern side of Liberia divides it from Côte d'Ivoire (formerly the Ivory Coast). This is a classic case of colonial borders splitting tribes down the middle, roping Krahn and Gio populations together in both countries. On the Côte d'Ivoire side, the Krahn and the Gio tribes have been living in harmony for centuries. In Liberia, they have been engaged in a genocidal war for five wars. The Krahn and the Gio in Côte d'Ivoire are hosting each other's refugees. It is possible (as I did a couple of years ago) to visit Côte d'Ivoire and visit one town where the Gios are hosting Gio refugees, and about an hour's drive down a dirt road, the Krahn are hosting Krahn refugees. Again, the Ivorian Krahn and the Ivorian Gio have been getting along fine. On the other side, they have been killing each other in huge numbers, so there must be another explanation for why the Krahn and the Gio tribes have been at war in Liberia.

A second example is South Africa. Many are familiar with what is sometimes referred to as "black on black" violence in South Africa. Much of it, particularly in the townships outside Johannesburg, has been between the Zulus and the Xhosas. Unfortunately, this conflict has been routinely characterized as a conflict that is based on ancient historic enmity between the Xhosas and the Zulus. In fact, there has been no history of conflict between the Xhosas and the Zulus in South Africa. Over the course of the many centuries of terrible violence in South Africa, the Xhosas and the Zulus are practically the only tribes in South Africa that have never fought each other. On the other hand, the two tribes that have had by far the most vicious and brutal conflict in South Africa's history and the history of southern Africa have been the two white tribes, the English-speaking whites and the Afrikaners during the Boer War. Those two white tribes fought with a degree of destruction and brutality that has never been matched by any of the other tribes in South Africa. The question is, therefore, Why are the Xhosas and the Zulus fighting each other now, and more specifically, Why have they been fighting each other since 1990, the year that the African National Congress (ANC) was legalized in South Africa and Nelson Mandela was released from prison?

It is also important to note that none of these tribes in any part of Africa have ever had any kind of conflict comparable with the conflicts in this century between, for example, the Germans and the French, or the Germans and the Russians. It is not conflict itself that feeds further conflict. Other elements must be in the equation. The single element in every conflict in all of these countries in Africa, both in what has until recently been characterized as Black Africa and South Africa, is the same common denominator that one finds in conflicts in the heart of Europe in this century—tyranny. These conflicts flow from calculated tyranny. In every case, unaccountable despots are making political calculations of their own self-interests.

What has been happening in South Africa and throughout Black Africa since the beginning of the Cold War is that despots have drawn their support from one of the two superpowers or from Western European powers. Those despots who derived their legitimacy from their role as proxies in the Cold War conflict have had the props that supported their regimes kicked out from under them. Mobutu in Zaire was a famous proxy of the United States. Throughout the Cold War, Habyarimana in Rwanda was a proxy of the French, and Daniel arap Moi in Kenya was a proxy agent both of the Americans and the British. All across Africa, these gangsters have had to shift to a new plan to hold on to power. Playing the ethnic card is an old tactic. As Harold Isaacs put it: "There is a constant flux in power relationships, and regarding the struggle of who is up and who is down, the most effective basis for mobilizing support remains the bedrock of group identity." This pattern exists in all of these different conflicts.

To demonstrate the machinations at play that are pitting different ethnic groups against each other, I will begin with Rwanda. It is a current and particularly vivid example of absolutely wanton, incomprehensible savagery and brutality. Rwanda also possesses all of the elements that are present in all of these other countries.

The first element is basic criminality. Most of the regimes in countries throughout Africa that have been embroiled in ethnic conflict have been governed by what could be characterized as criminal regimes—criminal in the literal sense of the word. Most of these governments are essentially criminal racketeering enterprises. The model that can be used to explain their conduct and to understand their interests is not an exotic model or a cultural model. It is basically the model of organized crime.

In the case of Rwanda, the president of Rwanda, Juvénal Habyarimana was killed in the plane crash of 6 April 1994. That plane crash triggered the genocide. Juvénal Habyarimana was the archetype of the African "big man" in every sense, including the fact that he was, among other things, a thug. He ran his government as a criminal, racketeering enterprise. His rackets were threefold. First, he was engaged in marijuana smuggling. Marijuana fields could be found all over the lush, green, tropical mountain slopes of central Africa where Rwanda is situated. They were being harvested by soldiers who transported the crop by army helicopters and shipped it throughout Africa and overseas. A cut of the profits was going to Habyarimana, his tiny clan, and a circle of people from his tiny village.

The second racket Habyarimana ran was in the trafficking of mountain gorillas. Many people are familiar with the saga of Dian Fossey, the American scholar killed in 1985 who lived with the mountain gorillas. One of the principal suspects in that killing was Habyarimana's brother-in-law. Habyarimana's family and associates were engaged in trafficking the severed heads, hands, and feet of mountain gorillas.

The third principal racket that Habyarimana ran was in currency manipulation. Habyarimana's brother-in-law was the governor of the Central Bank in Rwanda, and he had another brother-in-law who ran the only black market permitted to operate in Rwanda. The price of the U.S. dollar in the Central Bank on the legal market was one dollar for one Rwandan franc. The price on the black market was $1.50. By manipulating the distinction between the two rates, they were able to make millions of dollars. In short, these men were, among other things, crude criminals.

Habyarimana also possessed another element that exists in all of these countries through Africa. He was a product of the old Belgian colonial regime like a much more famous head of state in Africa, Mobutu Sese Seko in Zaire, another former Belgian colony. Habyarimana and Mobutu both found their callings as soldiers in the old Belgian colonial army. This army was created with the express purpose of enforcing Belgian colonial rule–in other words, the subjugation of the native inhabitants of Zaire and Rwanda. These men therefore found their calling essentially as collaborators with the colonial regime. This second pattern exists in all of these countries. The cast of characters who are behind these conflicts are all unsavory characters, and their unsavoriness goes all the way back to their choice of careers.

Another example of this second pattern is Samuel Doe in Liberia, the famous 28-year-old master sergeant who toppled the old regime in Liberia. He was a soldier in the Liberian armed forces, which was basically a militia organized from street thugs, unemployed toughs, and illiterate gangsters who were armed, trained, and put in uniforms. Their basic duty was to enforce an exclusionary regime that controlled the native inhabitants. This cast of characters was thus inherently opportunistic and cynical with the goal of acquiring power and wealth through whatever means necessary.

In South Africa, the same thing happened in the so-called third force. In America, people tend to be suspicious of conspiracy theories, and rightly so, but in some parts of the world conspiracy theories turn out to be true. South Africa is one of them. This conspiracy theory was confirmed a month before the election last year. The story was eclipsed by the election itself, but it was confirmed by a judicial commission, the Goldstone Commission, that there was a "third force" in South Africa. This force was created within the white-led police force of South Africa. The essential role of the police in South Africa was to manufacture weapons and provide them to Inkatha–basically to harness the criminal element among illiterate Zulus in the townships and in rural Natal, provide them with training and weapons, and send them into battle as a proxy force in South Africa. Imagine a crime wave and violence taking place, and the police, instead of trying to prevent the crime from happening, are doing everything possible to stoke it and arm the criminals. This scenario was the real situation in South Africa. The term in South Africa for this situation is an Afrikaner term: *kleur teen kleur beginsel*; it is the "color-against-color principle." Basically it meant pitting one group of blacks against another and creating a dynamic of violence that would discredit and destabilize the African National Congress. Again, it is a pattern found all over Africa.

There is also a similar old Sudanese saying from the 19th century when Arab slave trade merchants dominated southern Sudan by playing one black African tribe against another. The Arabic term means "let the slave eat the slave." This term demonstrates the strategy used by Arab governments in northern Sudan to keep southern Sudan in a state of permanent anarchy. The way they did it was by arming different militias in the south, arming chiefs, arming warlords, arming criminals, and pitting them one against another, thus creating a dynamic of anarchy.

This second pattern raises another element in all of these conflicts–the phenomenon of indirect rule. Indirect rule was the basic strategy utilized by all of the colonial powers in Africa and elsewhere in the colonial world, including India. In this strategy a colonial power, which by necessity is only going to include a small number of its own agents on the ground in a given colonial state, basically delegates the tasks of governance, repression, collection, policing, and bureaucratic responsibilities to what are referred to as "loyal natives." This tradition was followed throughout all of the colonies, South Africa being a particularly vivid example. In South Africa the system of indirect rule was established by a colonial governor named Theophilus Shepstone, who was the old administrator of native affairs in the 19th century. A port town on the Indian Ocean coast of Natal is called Port Shepstone to this day. It is at the heart of the violence that continues in South Africa.

For those who may have formed an impression that all is now peace and light in South Africa and that there have been many miraculous developments in South Africa, they should know that the violence continues. In Natal in January 1995, 131 politically motivated murders occurred, most of them taking place in this region around Port Shepstone. The principal protagonists in the violence are the old chiefs.

Many tend to think of chiefs and traditional authorities in traditional systems of government as something ancient, exotic, and perhaps even innocent, but the chief systems throughout Africa were essentially unaccountable systems of government. One of the things the British and French discovered when they arrived in Africa was that they could use this system of chiefs to their own advantage. If they could figure out a way to control the chiefs, then the chief's subjects would follow what the chiefs told them to do. Thus, through money, blandishments, favors, and coercion when necessary, the chiefs became part of the system of colonial domination.

In the case of South Africa with the advent of apartheid, the chiefs in South Africa, including Chief Mangosuthu Buthelezi, became employees of the South African government. When the underground structures of the African National Congress and the United Democratic Front began the uprising in the townships in the mid-1980s, their primary targets were the chiefs, those associated with the chiefs, and those associated with the Homeland governments; in other words, those associated with what were perceived of as the structures of apartheid and repression. In many of these cases, these guys in South Africa were surrounded by what they call the *amabutho*, which are the traditional militias organized among primarily illiterate rural populations to do the bidding of the chiefs. The chiefs mobilized these *amabutho* as protection from the attacks of the African National Congress.

This pattern also exists in other parts of the world likewise embroiled in ethnic conflict, the most obvious example being Bosnia. Most of the political leaders who are behind the ethnic cleansing in Bosnia, for example, are former Communists. These former Communist *apparatchiks* and bureaucrats found their positions, power, and money-making capacity destabilized with the end of the Cold War and withdrawal of support from the Soviet Union. They resorted to the ethnic card, which in the case of Bosnia is referred to as nationalism. They began inciting nationalist sentiments and playing on the fears and apprehensions of their nationalist confederates.

Likewise on that point, in addition to Bosnia, brutal ethnic wars are being waged in the former Soviet states of central Asia. In looking at the cast of characters who are running the militias, the independence movements, and the nationalist struggles in these countries, one can see that nearly all of these characters are former Communist leaders who derived their authority and legitimacy from their affiliation with the old Communist regime in Moscow. When that support was withdrawn, they resorted to the ethnic card, or as the case may be, the religious card–whatever it took to surround themselves with people whose identity could be affiliated with theirs.

Again, another element found in all of these conflicts is the element of propaganda, particularly on the radio. In all of these countries, the most virulent kind of propaganda is found on radio, and in most of these countries, radio is the only source of information people have. When trying to comprehend the extent and wanton savagery of the violence, it is also important to remember that especially in Africa, the overwhelming majority of people in all of these countries (including South Africa) are illiterate. These people have no access to information besides the information that is propagated over the radio and by their political leaders, most of whom are affiliated with the central, criminal state.

I can provide a few examples to illustrate the radio propaganda. I will read some of the radio dispatches that were broadcast in Rwanda when I was there at the height of the genocide in June 1994. While the killing was still continuing, the radio would broadcast in the Kinyarwanda language. Rwanda is populated by Hutus and Tutsis. The Hutus are primarily cultivators; the Tutsis are primarily pastoralists. The Tutsis were the collaborators under the old colonial regime. They were the minority who were allied with the Belgian colonial forces. The Belgians together with the Tutsis instituted essentially a feudal regime–a brutal feudal regime. These are the memories that have been stirred up over and over again in the propaganda. The radio comes on with guitars strumming in the background. The announcer says he is speaking to "those who understand." It is sort of code language–"those who understand." Those people are the "sons of the cultivators," the Hutus. He says, "Beware of the sons of the pastoralists." These are the Tutsis. "Defend your rights and rise up," he says. "Defend your rights and rise up against those who would oppress you."

The radio broadcaster also said that the Tutsis were singing songs that amounted to "nothing but expressions of nostalgic figures of Tutsi monarchy." This central theme of the radio propaganda in Rwanda went back to 1990–the year of the end of the Cold War, the withdrawal of Western support for Habyarimana's regime in Rwanda, and pressure from the West (particularly from Western financial institutions) to democratize and open the political system. Also in 1990 in Rwanda, Tutsi-led insurgency was beginning. Therefore, Habyarimana's regime had its back against the ropes without its traditional base of support and was trying to figure out a way to mobilize the Hutu population against all of these various threats. The basic line of the propaganda was that the Tutsis were coming to reimpose feudalism by taking all of the Hutus' land and killing the Hutus–the Tutsis were evil. Radio broadcasts referred to the Tutsis over and over again as the cockroaches. Another term for the Tutsis is the *inkotanyi*. The *inkotanyi* was the 19th-century Tutsi militia that bludgeoned the Hutus into submission under Belgian rule. The line repeated day after day was meant to blur the line between the Tutsis of today and these 19th-century oppressors.

I got a sense of the impact this propaganda has as I returned to Rwanda later in the year on an assignment to write about Rwandan children. I spent a week both inside Rwanda and in Zaire talking to Hutu and Tutsi youth, some of them as young as 17 years old. I spent a great deal of time asking them to explain from their perspective why this war was happening, why they were in a refugee camp in Zaire, what caused this disaster in their lives, and why their parents died of cholera. In the case of Tutsis, one could interview children 10, 12, and 15 years old who had literally been pulled out of piles of massacred victims. These children have personally witnessed unspeakable horrors. They have actually witnessed their entire families–all of their relatives, brothers, sisters, fathers, mothers–and all of the members of their schools and communities hacked to death before their eyes. When I asked them why these horrors occurred, they recited verbatim the radio propaganda they had heard for years. They all talked about the *inyenzi* and the *inkotanyi*. Even the Tutsis talk about their own people as the *inyenzi* and the *inkotanyi*. They do not realize that these names and labels have been attached for political reasons to individual people. They think these things are just the reality of the world in which they live. These people are illiterate and lack any basis for evaluating independently the information fed to them over the radio.

Another example of Radio Rwanda was broadcast in the weeks leading up to the genocide. Radio Rwanda attributed to the Rwanda Patriotic Front (RPF), the rebel movement, an ideology that the radio characterized as ethnic purification. It urged the rebels to "renounce once and for all their ideology of the power struggle based on vengeance and revenge." The purpose was to implant in the minds of Rwandans that the rebels were really bent on ethnic purification.

For comparison purposes, try to imagine that in the immediate aftermath of the Oklahoma bombing in April 1995, all of the radio stations in the country began announcing that this bombing was the work of people from Michigan and a Michigan militia wanted to take over the country and destroy the government. Imagine the president and the attorney general repeating this announcement on the radio and saying that they were going to take the people from Michigan and kill them all because if they did not, the people from Michigan were going to kill others. Imagine further that the National Guard, the police forces, and the U.S. Army were all mobilized down to the state and local level in order to go after the Michigan militias and all of the people of Michigan who would presumably be allied with the Michigan militias. Then suppose that in fact in an earlier era of 10, 30, or 50 years ago, the people of Michigan did impose some sort of tyranny on the rest of the country, and that there is a history of racism and division between the people of Michigan and the rest of the Americans. Also add to this picture that Americans are overwhelmingly illiterate–there is no *New York Times* or "Nightline." There is only one radio station and only one talk radio host who is propagating this line about the people from Michigan. Then one can begin to imagine that things can get very ugly very quickly.

Propaganda is a phenomenon found in all of these different countries, including South Africa. In South Africa in the months leading up to the election last year, the Zulu language radio was broadcasting in Natal a message that was being carried to the hostels in the townships in the Transvaal. Chief Buthelezi repeated over and over again that one had to fight against the ANC. The critical element of the propaganda in South Africa being broadcast by the Zulu chiefs, Buthelezi, and Inkatha was against the ANC, the Xhosas. Buthelezi said the Zulus would be subjected to genocide, ethnic cleansing, and having their land taken. He was quoted as saying, "They want to leave us homeless so that we too will be forced to wander in the desert as the people of Israel did after their emancipation from Egypt."

I will conclude with a bottom line. People ask me what the solution is in Africa–whether any solution exists, or if Africa is destined to permanent anarchy and bloodshed. Fortunately, as a journalist, I am not paid to have bright ideas and rarely have them. The only recommendation I have for Africa is the same recommendation I have for all of the other parts of the world, which is to establish the rule of law and democracy–an idea hatched in the 18th century in part by Thomas Jefferson. This basis is actually what South Africa is now trying to accomplish. It is the only thing in my view that can set South Africa apart from all of the other countries of black Africa. The basic challenge is to try to hold accountable those who have been engaged in criminal violence in the past. I will not go into the details of the so-called truth and reconciliation commission, which is presently underway in South Africa, but the system of some sort of individual accountability for crimes is the only thing that can separate these countries from a situation where groups are pitted one against another.

QUESTION: You have been talking mainly about sub-Saharan Africa. Does Arab north Africa, specifically the regime of Libyan leader Gadhafi, fit into that mold?

MR. BERKELEY: I would hesitate to talk about Gadhafi. I have not been to Libya. I have suspicions, but I would say certainly from what I do know that he is basically a gangster, among other things. I do not know the exact machinations he uses to hold on to power. Libya has a great deal more money than many of these countries, which means there is more money to spread around. The carrot is almost always more effective than the stick. Many times the stick becomes necessary when the resources of carrots run out.

QUESTION: Considering that television has only existed for less than 50 years, do you think the situation you have described has gotten worse during the last 50 years, or does the world just know more about what has been happening in Africa?

MR. BERKELEY: I think people know more about what is happening. A million people died in the Biafra War in Nigeria in the 1960s. At least a million were killed in Uganda in the 1970s. Half a million died in Sudan between 1955 and 1973. The Belgians in the old Belgian Congo in the early part of this century killed untold millions of native inhabitants of that area. I do not think that the problem has gotten worse in terms of dynamics. One element has changed and has raised the stakes and the casualty figures–the introduction of modern armaments. The armaments have made the cycle of violence much more destructive and difficult to arrest. Automatic weapons kill far more people than simple implements. Therefore, if someone can arm a militia in southern Sudan with AK-47 rifles, it is that much more difficult to arrest the cycle because the violence has been that much more destructive. So yes, the casualty figures perhaps have risen from direct violence as opposed to famine, but these kinds of things have been happening for a long time. I really do not think that in terms of ethnicity it has gotten worse.

Another difference is that in the past, people tended to think of these conflicts as Cold War conflicts and projected their own labels–freedom fighters, Communists, allies, or enemies–on the different protagonists. They failed to realize that in fact, ethnicity was at the core or that the principal political figures were basically warlords. With the removal of the Cold War as an explanation and the removal of the various ideologies of the Cold War as explanations, it has become more obvious that more basic issues are in play.

QUESTION: Your thesis that large-scale violence is normally caused or instigated by criminal tyrants is fascinating. It is less clear why and how this mechanism operates or why tyrannical governments would regard having a society driven into chaos by violence to be to their advantage. I can imagine circumstances in which it is, but I think if I were a criminal tyrant I might want a placid society rather than one that was driven into anarchy by internal violence. Why wouldn't, in many cases, tyrants undertake to stabilize their society rather than to destroy it?

MR. BERKELEY: The answer is that sometimes they do, and very often the tyrants who fail to make that sort of calculation live to regret it. One might have thought Hitler would have made a calculation that it was unwise to attack the Soviet Union. Undoubtedly, he regretted this move. One may think Saddam Hussein would have made the calculation that it would be unwise first to attack Iran and then to challenge the United States. Tyrants make mistakes.

In Rwanda, although it was Habyarimana's regime that created the apparatus of genocide, he was a shrewd operator who evidently made the calculation that it was unwise to unleash that machinery of genocide. Then he was killed. The most common explanation for the killing of President Habyarimana was that he was making compromises that would threaten his and his allies' positions.

The answer is therefore that some individuals make individual calculations. Mobutu in Zaire is another classic example. He has clearly made a calculation that if he can simply eliminate the state and create a situation of anarchy because Zaire is so diffuse, spread out, and underdeveloped that he and his supporters would benefit from the chaos. Most of these despots, like most gangsters, generally make the calculation that carrots are generally more effective than sticks. Violence is unpredictable, and they do the best they can to spread money around.

In Kenya, Daniel arap Moi simply printed money at the time of the elections that were imposed on him a couple of years ago. Using his agents in the Central Bank, he increased the money supply by 33 percent in six months and created 100 percent inflation simply to pay off all of his various agents, operatives, candidates, and so forth. By means of blandishments and bribes, he sought to buy his way back into power, and he succeeded. Some people get desperate, and some people fail to foresee the consequences of violence.

The one element of the equation I would like to highlight that I did not mention comes from the question of why, for example, South Africa, after 15,000 to 20,000 deaths, seems to be arresting the cycle. It has not gone up in flames. Likewise, after serious violence in Kenya, everyone predicted Kenya was going to go the way of its neighbors, which it has not done. Why not? Why have these countries not gone up in flames?

The central point that distinguishes both Kenya and South Africa even to a larger degree from the others is the existence of the middle class. Whereas sometimes individual gangsters and their little cliques of criminal collaborators often miscalculate their interests and what it will take to hold on to power, an educated middle class tends to be a better vehicle for making rational calculations. A middle class also tends to make the calculation that the rule of law is in their best interests. In Kenya, the tribe that has been most provoked by political violence in the last several years has been the Kikuyu. They also are predominant in the middle class. Many of them have a stake in stability, and as a group led by educated elites, they made a calculation that it would be unwise to destabilize their country and go the way of their neighbors.

Likewise in South Africa, white South Africans led by the business people in South Africa in the 1980s first began putting pressure on the Afrikaner old guard to start making compromises. White South Africa was a form of group tyranny, not individual tyranny. White South Africa was a well-educated, predominately middle-class grouping. Considerable debate is taking place in the press. South Africa is relentlessly documenting all of the abuses that are occurring and the violence taking place. As a group, white South Africans basically made the sound calculation that it would be counterproductive to their own interests to continue down the path of unending war.

QUESTION: On the question of education, the rule of law is never going to apply to anyone that is uneducated because they do not have the capacity to reason. Are any efforts in place in any of these countries to educate the people?

MR. BERKELEY: I did not make reference to it, but it is in fact occurring. In many of the countries I have been discussing, they have either been at war for many years or they have been governed by despots who are simply thinking about how to make money. They are not thinking about how to improve the lot of the people. Therefore, no development, education, or prospect of an improved dispensation will occur while war continues.

Kenyans, for example, tend to be the best-educated people, and the Kikuyu are the best educated, in part, going back to the British colonial era. British colonialism in east Africa was a mixed bag.

It is a sad picture for the future. For example, Uganda went through absolutely the worst nightmare in the 1970s and early 1980s under Idi Amin and Milton Obote. The new head of state, however, is a man named Yoweri Museveni. His strategy for preventing Uganda from sliding back into anarchy is economic development and the creation of an educated middle class, which, as he puts it, can create horizontal linkages between different groups as distinguished from the vertical ties of ethnicity. So in some countries, resources do exist, and certainly education is a priority. Zimbabwe is another example. The government of Zimbabwe has problems and Zimbabwe is by no means perfect, but it did make educating its people a priority, beginning with independence in 1980.

NARRATOR: We have certainly learned a great deal from Mr. Berkeley's discussion, and we are grateful to him for sharing his considerable knowledge with us.

CHAPTER TWO

Collapsed States in Africa*

I. WILLIAM ZARTMAN

NARRATOR: William Zartman is Jacob Blaustein Professor of International Organization and Conflict Resolution and director of African Studies at the Paul H. Nitze School of Advanced International Studies. He has a master's degree from Johns Hopkins and a doctorate degree from Yale.

Mr. Zartman has taught at many African and Middle Eastern universities, including the American University in Cairo, the University of Damascus, the University of Algiers, the University of Ghana, the University of the Cameroons, the University of Zaire, and the University of Somalia. He has written several books on North Africa and on the subject of negotiation, including *Government and Politics in North Africa, International Relations in the New Africa, Africa in the 1980's, Ripe for Resolution: Conflict and Intervention in Africa, The 50% Solution, Positive Sum: Improving North-South Negotiations, The Practical Negotiator*, and *International Mediation in Theory and Practice.*

Dr. Zartman helped shape the international peacemaking program at the International Peace Academy. He also initiated courses on negotiations in the State Department's Foreign Service Institute. Dr. Zartman has received numerous awards and grants from such organizations as the Rockefeller Foundation, the Social Science Research Council, the National Science Foundation, and the National Endowment for the Humanities. He has been an

---

**Presented in a Forum at the Miller Center of Public Affairs on 8 August 1994.*

officer of the Fulbright Council and also a member of the American Council of Learned Societies Joint Committee on the Near and Middle East. In 1993-94 he was Olin Professor at the U.S. Naval Academy.

Dr. Zartman's thesis on collapsed states is that the breakdown of authority creates and opens the door to ethnic conflict. His thesis challenges the view that sees causality operating in the other direction, that ethnic conflict in many of the African states is the cause, rather than the result, of the breakdown of states such as Rwanda and Somalia.

Hopes were bright in the 1960s. Nigeria, for example, thanks to the British, had a foreign and civil service and seemed to be doing very well. Other countries, one of which has recently gone down badly–the Ivory Coast–seemed to be booming in terms of their growth rate and their development. Unfortunately, hopes burn less brightly today. In a recent World Bank report only one African country was listed as adequate in terms of its growth and development, namely, Ghana. We welcome Dr. Zartman to discuss the topic of collapsed states in Africa.

MR. ZARTMAN: I would like to begin by establishing three points that I will be addressing in my presentation. The first point is that *collapsed states* is a concept to be distinguished from a state simply having trouble with government, rebellions, overthrows, or other such occurrences. Second, I will present a kind of model for why states collapse. Although I will not have time to present the model in full detail because of its complexity, I would like to outline the main causes of state collapse. Third, I will propose some solutions for what to do when states are in the process of collapsing and how they can be put back together.

The first point is that collapse is a separate phenomenon from a coup or a rebellion or troubles with government. When we talk about collapsed states, we are talking about a breakdown of law and order, of legitimate authority. It is difficult for us in our comfortable American settings to think about what would happen when there is no government or state present in the territory, nothing to which one can turn to establish legitimate rules of authority or of law and order. This situation is very different from someone taking over the structures of a state from another person, even by unconstitutional means. In that situation, the structures continue to exist. There is a short interregnum and a fight for legitimate authority, but the authority structures themselves are not gone. In a collapsed state, all possibility of creating law, order, and legitimacy disappears.

A collapsed state is not necessarily a situation of anarchy. Law and order may be located somewhere other than the centralized structure of the state; for example, they might be located in local structures of authority. Thus, we find in the situation of collapse that power often devolves to local centers, even grass-roots structures of civil society that take over functions of the state. Consequently, when state collapse occurs, one may not have bandit groups or civil war, but rather just an absence of a center, an absence of anyone who exercises recognized authority over the state.

To illustrate this concept and its causes and remedies, I will focus mainly on African cases because these are the cases I know best. Moreover, Africa happens to be a continent in which there are a number of collapsed states. At the same time, it should be noted that collapse is not a condition of African states in general. Some African states are doing very well, and others have collapsed and come back. Therefore, when we say collapsed states, I certainly do not mean that all of the states of Africa are somewhere in the process of collapse. Afro-pessimism is a wave sweeping our media these days. When we think of Africa at all, we think of it in bad terms, ignoring the fact that much in Africa is quiet, stable, and still functioning.

Neither do I mean to say that collapse of states is a phenomenon that will sweep the world in the coming future, in our lives or our children's lives, as in the writings of Robert Kaplan who has suggested that it is a portender of what lies ahead for all of us. To the contrary, it is a selective phenomenon, a special phenomenon that takes place according to identifiable patterns and for specific reasons; it is not something that is likely to characterize the condition of the whole world ahead of us.

The Cases

The collapse of states in Africa has taken place in waves since the beginning of independence. These incidences tell us something about the nature of the phenomenon, its causes and its relation to what else is going on in the world. When we think of state collapse in Africa–if our memories go back that far–we think of the Congo events, the events that took place in a country now called Zaire in the early 1960s. Although they took place in Africa, the events of the Congo were not typical of Africa and were not typical of collapsed states. They rather marked the collapse of a colonial regime that had not prepared for its successor and were a unique occurrence in the history of African (and most other) decolonization.

The first wave of collapse in the African continent took place in the late 1970s, where a number of states similar in nature fell apart and their governments simply disappeared for a number of years. Examples are cases such as Uganda at the end of Idi Amin's rule, Chad at the end of François Tombalbaye's rule, possibly Mauritania after Moktar Ould Daddah's rule, and even events that took place in Ghana at the end of a number of different types of regimes in which government by the late 1970s, in the interlude between the two Rawlings coups, lost its authority over the country and was unable to make policy and carry it out. Ghana is not a case of total collapse, but there are aspects characteristic of the phenomenon in general. In short, a number of cases at the end of the 1970s were marked for the most part by a strong man who had seized power and then had so narrowed the scope of power by gathering it together in a single hand that it fell apart and became irreplaceable for a period of time.

The next wave of collapse took place a decade later at the end of the 1980s, foreshadowing many of today's events. One might say either that this wave prepared for a third wave or that the 1980s wave has just continued into the middle of the 1990s. Here we know of the cases: Somalia, where a government fell apart as once more a dictator gathered power for a small number of people and then, weakened by an auto accident, was finally overthrown by a rebellion that spread throughout the country and no one could restore the government; Liberia, where a strong man had concentrated power, again to the point where he began to alienate the rest of the country so that once the revolt began, it spread like wildfire throughout the countryside, stopping just outside the walls of the capital–this government fell completely apart as the dictator, Samuel Doe, was cut into pieces on television, yet the rebellion still unable to take over and restore power; or Rwanda, the current case, much like the case of Liberia, where the ruler in power for a long time suddenly disappeared and the rebellion was kept from taking power, resulting in the collapse of all law and order.

Other cases illustrate how government, or some semblance of government or authority, has remained but is ineffective throughout the country until finally the extension of its power is reduced and confined simply to the capital–all this without a rebellion ever taking place. Examples are cases like Mozambique or Angola. Still other cases such as Ethiopia show how a rebellion might finally take over government and yet still remain unable to make it run effectively. Many similarities exist among these very different cases. Somalia, Liberia, and Rwanda are instances of total collapse in our present time, while Angola, Mozambique, and Ethiopia are instances with only some of the characteristics of collapse.

Perhaps more frightening are the cases hanging on the edges of our news media, cases that have many of the same characteristics just described and are just waiting to happen. Burundi, for example, has already had some massacres on the scale of a small Rwanda last year as the first elected president took office. It is now in a state of frozen rebellion as the military is able to keep a lid on dissidents within the general population; however, this military lid is little more than a means of artificial control and is therefore likely to break apart soon.

In Zaire a similar situation is taking place. A military leader who has been in power for nearly 30 years is approaching the end of his reign, and like the earlier cases mentioned, Zaire's government is simply not functioning throughout the country. Last year, Amnesty International said that Zaire, as a state, is in a state of collapse. The state of Zaire has not completely disappeared in the sense of which we have been talking because there is still a government in the capital. Nevertheless, its final disintegration will hit the screens in a year or two, much as it has in Somalia, Liberia, and Rwanda.

Other incomplete cases include Sierra Leone, where a half-hearted military coup overthrew the government but is nevertheless unable to exercise authority throughout the country. Similarly, Algeria, where the government has been unable to function since 1988, has been completely preoccupied with questions of law and order. Algeria is simply unable to fulfill normal government policy functions.

An interesting case that did not happen, but was set up to take place, was South Africa. There an illegitimate government was trying to devise ways by which it could hand power over to a legitimate successor by way of a process made illegitimate by the participation of that government. Meanwhile, extreme groups on the right and left and in both the black and white parts of the community were challenging the law and order functions of the government in power. The country made it through that crisis, but again there are characteristics that help us examine the phenomenon of state collapse.

Finally, as a possibility for the future, there is the case of Sudan, where the government, unable to rule half the country, has pulled itself together–not around a small ethnic elite or a family as in Somalia, but around a religious interpretation of its calling and by that process is losing a great deal of support within the country. By trying to be strong, it has become narrower and weaker. A government still exists in Sudan and still makes a credible claim to rule the country, but the credibility of its rule applies to only part of the country; collapse is setting in.

In sum, there are a number of clear-cut cases of collapse as well as cases of partial collapse that tell us something about the phenomenon. A whole series of cases are also waiting to happen–Zaire, Burundi, Sierra Leone, and possibly Sudan.

The Causes

Why does collapse take place, and what is involved in this phenomenon? First, a general answer that simply reinforces the concept is that collapse takes place because the state can no longer perform the functions expected of it as a state. Why can't it do this? What is the process that leads to collapse? The "why" question is better answered as a "how" question: How does collapse take place?

Before turning to the "how," there is another answer to the "why" question that has been proposed and of which I would like to dispose. It is often said that collapse takes place in Africa because the state is inappropriate to the African condition. I have been limiting myself to Africa in my examples, but state collapse has occurred in other places such as Cambodia, Afghanistan, and Lebanon, for example—cases outside of Africa, making it hard to say that the Western state is not an appropriate form of government for a particular region. I think this answer is inadequate—even a wrong answer—because it applies the notion of "Western" to a phenomenon of governance that is universal. Political systems or societies have had to devise means of providing law and order for their social organization as well as a legitimate structure in whose name they can operate. Although there are situations of leaderless societies, nonstate societies of which Africa has many examples, these are small-scale societies. Large-scale societies the size of even a small state—a Togo or a Gambia—require a state type of structure. It is inadequate to say that states collapse in Africa because they do not belong there or because a state is not an appropriate African structure. The fact is that by whatever name you call it, a state is required. Structures are needed to provide legitimate authority and law and order, and it is not the nature of the beast itself that is wrong; rather, it is the way that the animal is put together.

Two types of processes are involved in collapse. Collapse takes place by a downward spiral of debilitating practices within a government and then eventually within the state. In the examples mentioned, a central authority concentrates power and benefits into a smaller and smaller group, until finally it operates in the name, and for the benefit, of a particular referent group within society. In the process of gathering power, the central authority provokes opposition from people who claim that they deserve part of the benefits as well; however, instead of treating the opposition as legitimate demand-bearing groups, the central authority treats opposition as an illegitimate attack on government and tries to repress it. The more it represses, the more it pushes parts of society into opposition, not simply against government but against the entire state structure associated with the government. Thus, a narrowing process of the state takes place while the state simultaneously turns against parts of society that it has cut off from its own exercise and from policy benefits. The state alienates society as it goes on retreating into its castle. The state on the verge of collapse is a state that is holed up within its fortress, governing for the benefit of a small group of people while all of the fields and peasants remain outside–not simply outside the walls of the fortress, but alienated from government itself. That state then depends on the people who man the castle to keep law and order within a repressive structure. When that structure in turn collapses, there is nothing left. There is a vacuum in the center. Not only do the occupants of the castle, the wielders of authority, have to be replaced, but the notions of legitimacy within that state have to be recreated–the notions that give right to rulership within the society.

A downward spiral collapse does not occur as a gradual movement but rather happens in stages, frequently involving a succession of military rulers after an original civilian rule fails in its task. It may involve, as it did in Ghana, an alteration of military and civilian rule, but at each of these stages the functions of keeping order in society and providing programs and outputs within a society are less and less well performed. Thus, I would like to suggest an alternative to viewing the process of state collapse as a downward spiral. Instead, one might view state collapse as an object falling down a set of steps. Like the cars that sometimes fall off a cliff in the movies, the state slowly falls until it hits something and then rests there for a minute before slowly toppling down to the next level and the next, until finally it stops at the bottom of the chasm.

This kind of falling is something many polities do. One government functions poorly, a military rule takes over in reaction to the inadequacies or to some grievance against government, and then it bounces back (unlike in the movies). It gathers itself together, and civil society comes back again in support of the government. People begin to believe that this time things will be better. In a process of winning legitimacy and the support of the population, of gathering together the inputs necessary for government and returning them back to the population via its policies, a government is able to pick itself up and bounce back up.

When collapse takes place, however, at no point is that rebounding able to take place. At no step is the government able to rally popular support, to get civil society to contribute legitimacy, candidates, or policy supports behind the government. It bounces down and down to the bottom. Thus, if we want to understand the process of collapsed states and look ahead to the future, we have to look at the entire process, not just the last bounce. Collapse does not take place at the last minute, but rather through the process of weakening government and weakening state legitimacy over a longer period of time.

There is a special twist that seems common among the cases just discussed; that is, the last step downward involves a rebellion and a new leader. He may not be any better than his predecessor, but at least he enters with a good deal of support and relief from the population because he has removed the tyrant of the moment and has promised some kind of change. That situation is normal and happens frequently. In the cases that have provoked state collapse, however, that takeover of power by a rebellion with a presumption of support by the population is stopped, blocked by international intervention or by the inadequacy of the rebellion. For some reason or other, instead of taking over with the initial legitimacy from having destroyed the tyrant, that attempt is stopped in its tracks and collapse occurs.

The examples are many. In Somalia, for instance, a tyrant was overthrown. Someone attempted to set up a new system for the benefit of a number of parts of the Somali nation, not first the clan of Siad Barre, but suddenly at the last step he found himself countered by another person planning to take over; thus, the war between Ali Mahdi and Mohamed Aideed broke out, blocking the takeover. Because each blocked the other's attempt to enter the door of legitimate power, a power vacuum occurred in the middle instead.

Another example is Charles Taylor in Liberia. As he was about to take power, a faction of his movement broke away under Prince Johnson—the person who cut up Samuel Doe—and then the Nigerian-led Ecomog forces blocked what seemed like a new government that would restore authority for the benefit of at least the larger group of the population. Somewhat lesser cases occurred in Angola and Mozambique, where government was awful, incapable, and losing its control over the countryside. In these cases, replacement rebellion did not take place—not because of foreign intervention, but because of its own inadequacies. Thus, a number of cases with this special twist have occurred in which an inability to restore law and order and state functions resulted in a vacuum in the center and hence the collapse of the state.

Other characteristics of state collapse provide additional material that is interesting and important to note when looking to reconstitute the state. One characteristic has to do with political space and another with economic space—characteristics moving in opposite directions. I have said that in times of state collapse, authority often devolves to the local level, either in a venal fashion—as warlords—or as a local authority. Society does pull together, but it does so at the local level rather than the national level. There are still pieces of authority in the country at the moment of state collapse that could provide the building blocks necessary for reconstituting the state, but some conundrums also exist.

On the other hand, political space often extends beyond the country's borders, as opposition leaders often leave to play politics on national political space from abroad. As a result, the political space—the area in which politics are played—often extends beyond the country itself, and major leaders wait on the borders or try to extend their claim of control over that vacuum.

In economic terms, economic space is often hived off to neighboring economies, often to the point where national currencies of the neighboring country are used within the collapsed state. During the long Ethiopian war that led to the collapse of the Ethiopian state, for example, economic business continued to thrive.

The economy kept functioning while the war continued, but it functioned as a part of the Somali economy, the Kenyan economy, and the Ugandan economy–that is, it functioned as pieces of neighboring economies that impinged on what was before a national Ethiopian economy. Moreover, it was natural that it should turn out this way because the central control of the economy had eroded as a part of state collapse. Similarly, in Zaire today, people use the Zambian kwacha or the currency of other neighboring countries because the currency of Zaire is not worth anything. Thus, the restoration of collapsed states involves getting the economy back from the enclaves of neighboring countries.

As this downward step process ends and collapse reaches its final paroxysm, a number of features characteristic of state collapse are evident. For example, not only does power pull back into the castle, but people within the castle begin fighting amongst themselves for power in that last stage of state collapse. Power disintegrates as the center fights amongst itself. Often what happens, then, is the withering away of the state by default so that its referent group, its social base, ends up being only the people in the castle; that is, the Marchan clan within the Darod faction of Somalis, or the Krahn people in Liberia. The state malfunctions not only as a law and order organism, but also as a policy body. The state is unable to make tough decisions for one of two reasons: institutional malfunction, where the legislature and executive get so caught up in the game of checks and balances that nothing is produced; or political incompetence. The leader at the top simply is unable to make decisions, but an attempt to replace him brings down the whole system.

As a result, politics become defensive. Instead of introducing a program or holding regular legitimizing elections, even if they are plebiscites, measures are taken to keep opponents out of the castle and its benefits; and politics, as a result, simply becomes a way of holding off opponents who are declared to be illegitimate.

Finally, the last mark of state collapse frequently is the corruption of those who are supposed to represent legitimate authority; that is, the agents of law and order become the problem of law and order. The tax collector collects taxes for himself. The person who terrorizes the local village is the local policemen or the local army unit. Because they are not paid by the center, they therefore depend on their own abilities–with the help of their uniforms and guns–to collect money for living expenses. These characteristics seem to typify the state's final bounce before it hits rock-bottom and the center proves to be a vacuum.

The Cures

Unfortunately, I do not have a solution to this eternal, long-term political problem. I can, however, point out some functions that need to be restored. We can then take these specific measures and cases and put them in conceptual baskets. I will also point out some traps that ought to be considered and addressed.

As policy is examined, one has to avoid confusing bad policy with good policy that is just badly implemented. Much of our debate–just as a side jab at Haiti today–reflects a confusion between what is clearly bad policy and what is badly implemented good policy. One must keep in mind some of the problems that can arise in the implementation of appropriate policy, lest good policy be undermined by our confusing the details of its implementation with the policy itself.

Putting a state back together requires the restoration of the functions the state had been unable to perform because the state's inability to perform those functions is what created the vacuum in the center. Political structures, legitimacy, resources, and peace can be considered the four components of state restoration necessary to end the fighting.

In restoring legitimate structures, a major problem exists. Restoring legitimate structures means putting people who are able to exercise authority back into institutions of government. The question is, however, who is best qualified to serve? On the one hand, one might draw from the local warlords–people who had seized power when power was up for grabs but who had been able to exercise that power only at the local level. These warlords are powerful but unworthy, however, because they were part of the initial problem. On the other hand, the institutions might be filled with representatives of civil society–lawyers, doctors, elders, and religious leaders–who are respected but who hid to avoid being killed when the fighting began or the collapse occurred. Such people, however, do not have the hard nerves necessary to exercise power. Perhaps the best solution for effective and legitimate government is to bring the two groups together. People must recognize that those who created the problem are also part of the solution. At the same time, political structures must be restored in a manner that does not allow them to have too much power. Thus, the talents of civic leaders are also involved in building political structures.

On the question of restoring legitimacy, restoring a government that is worthy of support is not enough; it must also be a government that benefits from the mechanisms of support. Only one mechanism of support exists, namely, popular support that can express itself via an election, a referendum, or a plebiscite. Interestingly, when military regimes come to power, no matter who they are in the world, they feel illegitimate until they have had an election of some kind, even if it is rigged. Military regimes inherently need that kind of legitimization. But again, should an election be called early, thus allowing for a plebiscite on a new ruler and avoiding divisions, or should there be a democratic election that allows for infighting, competition, or divisions among local groups or ethnic groups?

Part of an answer is that a winner-take-all election should not be called because such an election would automatically create some outs. A better answer to the dilemma is an election in which all parties participate, and which results in the apportionment of power. Power-sharing is still better, even though it means a softening of the accountability function of elections at the initial stages, because it gives the government legitimacy. Elections determine who should hold power, but elections can come only after the re-creation of the state, since structures for elections do not exist if a state does not exist.

The problem of a central vacuum is that no one has resources or a way of extracting resources for redistribution to society. New people claiming to represent legitimate structures have to reward followers in some way or else they will have no followers. Thus, they need immediate resources. The trap involved is whether resources, which necessarily have to come from the outside, can be kept as leverage until the government gets started without becoming habit-forming. A new government that depends on external resources from the beginning can become so dependent on outside sources of economic goods that it never generates goods within its own society. External support is needed for a new government, but with deadlines or time limits so that it does not become habit-forming.

Finally, what is needed is an operation that restores peace and the possibility of normalcy to society so that state institutions can be set up. All four components of state restoration–political structures, legitimacy, resources, and peace–point to something important in policy terms; that is, restoring a collapsed state necessitates external intervention. It can be done over a long period of time without external intervention but only at tremendous cost and only in a world that is bigger, less communicating, and less aware than the world in which people are now living. Today we cannot bear the cost of wars being fought to their ultimate end. We cannot endure the cost of a country without state authority. To move the process relatively expeditiously, there has to be an external role in these functions, but external roles, by their very nature, are wrong. A state cannot be set up through someone else. Legitimacy cannot be provided from the outside, unless there is an imperial system throughout the world. There is a basic contradiction in restoring states with external help. The way out of that contradiction is to operate under a simple two-handed guideline that says external intervention must stay as long as it is needed but leave as soon as it can. A double commitment has to be made as soon as possible with the provision that the external presence remain only as long as it is required.

We are left with a number of conundrums and contradictions as to what goes into policy decisions, but also with a number of ways of thinking about a phenomenon that people often take for granted yet has disappeared from some places of the world–namely, the legitimate exercise of law and order through established authority structures.

NARRATOR: What do you think of Professor Mazrui's idea that the outside force to which you referred in your conclusion could be recolonialization–not by the former colonial powers, but by Ethiopia or states that have made some headway in grappling with some of these issues and thus have experience of their own in struggling with collapsed states?

MR. ZARTMAN: I think we have to be careful in considering the recolonialization idea. Mazrui threw out many exciting ideas, but he is often not careful about some of the implications of his remarks. We have to be careful in understanding colonialism. Colonialism involved transferring the skills of the colonizer to the colonized to the point where the colonized could govern themselves. It involved a kind of love-hate relationship where in the end the colonized kicked out the colonizer. A prescription for recolonializing as a cure for state collapse means that colonialization would take place rapidly rather than over the long term. Long-term colonialization is empire-building, and Mazrui is not suggesting that there be an Ethiopian empire over the Horn of Africa. He is talking about a trusteeship for the moment. The effective operation of a trusteeship means that you are going to be hated and kicked out. The act of kicking out the colonizers symbolizes a country's readiness to take up its own destiny. In the short run such a trusteeship involves none of the economic benefits that colonialization usually provides–for example, the benefits and transferral of skills bestowed upon colonies during the first half of this century. Moreover, it place the colonizing state in the position of being disliked even more by its neighbor than at the present time. It is hard for Ethiopia to be disliked more by Somalia than it is right now. If states think through the process, I doubt if they would take this approach.

The other part of your question refers to cases Mazrui cited. Ethiopia is not yet completely safe from its own possible collapse. It is in no position to take over Somalia and put it back together. As for Ghana, I do not know what country it is going to take over, but it is not going to take over Nigeria. The addition of Nigeria, in fact, completes my list of states that face impending collapse. Nigeria is in real difficulty at the present time and illustrates the analogy that I made earlier when I compared state collapse to falling down the stairs of devolving government functions–the increasingly worse performance of government functions over the last decade and more.

The genius of colonialization was that it was a system not only of local order but of world order as well. It brought in people whom the locals had not yet learned to hate. In fact, the locals initially accepted and imitated them. The colonizer brought a new way of life. Ethiopians are not going to bring a new way of life to the Somalis.

QUESTION: What do you regard as the normal state of mankind, order or anarchy? Which would surprise us more, the existence of a stable regime or the absence of it?

MR. ZARTMAN: The absence of one, although it depends on what you mean by normal. If you mean political original sin or something going back philosophically to the beginning, selfish man has difficulty living in society. That problem was resolved conceptually in the 18th century when people thought about the social contract and the various ways of making it. The normal condition by any kind of measure today is law and order. I think if one looks simplistically for normality in the world today, the normal condition is functioning states.

Malfunctioning states is human normalcy; that is, people do not do anything perfectly, but at least it is normalcy in that there are functioning systems, even though they do not work very well. State collapse is an aberration in my opinion, and that is an abnormal function.

QUESTION: Could you discuss more thoroughly the Robert Kaplan thesis that not only will collapsed states and anarchy be seen in increasing numbers, but also that they will take place in areas where the United States has much greater interest? Concerning the Middle East, Kaplan is very worried about what the future of Iraq and other states in that region will be like. Kaplan is even more worried about the pieces of the former Soviet Union.

MR. ZARTMAN: I was horrified by the Kaplan article, which was one of the worst pieces of writing I have ever seen. Kaplan is like a person who looks at the countryside and says, "Those two trees–they line up if you look at them in a certain way. That is a portender that all trees could be lined up if you looked at them in a certain way." With that observation, he then turns to something else.

Kaplan says that Iraq is an awful state, and just think what would happen if every other state were like Iraq. On what basis did he make that statement? Nothing in the article convinced me that I should think of all other states being like Iraq. I cannot grapple with his proofs because I do not see any there. Instead, I see the state as the normal order of society–why shouldn't a state continue to function? States will function in different ways because they become more permeable, but there are many interstate activities that continue to be regulated by the state. Consider the health debate, for example. We should remind ourselves how much the state regulates. Though Kaplan identifies some real challenges, I do not see that type of governing breaking down. To my mind, the population challenge is enormous, but to jump from there to the conclusion that there will be a generalized collapse of states seems like a jump over a bridge that Kaplan has yet to draw. State collapse does happen, but only in a small number of identifiable cases. What in my own scenario proves that state collapse will remain isolated to a small number of states? I do not have the answer yet, and I will have to wrestle with that question some more. Nevertheless, I do not find the proof in what Kaplan has said.

QUESTION: The steps identified for rebuilding a state were essentially those that the United Nations tried in Somalia, at least in principle. What do you think accounts for the U.N.'s failure in that country?

MR. ZARTMAN: First, we have not yet failed. A good deal of success in building and restoring legitimate local functions to district councils has occurred, so that now local government has spread throughout much of Somalia, even if it is not coordinated under a national structure. We were waylaid on the awful Aideed affair, which I think was a good policy carried out badly. Meanwhile, Aideed was strengthened by having thumbed his nose at the great authorities of the world. The United Nations was weakened; therefore the potential and organization of the outside helper were rendered more powerless. The U.N.'s failure was in not being able to constitute an accepted national authority. The United Nations did not have enough of a plan to carry the periodic meetings in Addis in 1993 to an agreed national structure. It did not have enough punishments for failure. Neither did it have enough of a long-term goal for bringing the parties together. Nevertheless, the United Nations was successful in that it restored hope by bringing food to the Somalis, lowered the level of violence at the national level, and built up local authority.

QUESTION: What will be the future of Sudan?

MR. ZARTMAN: I see only two main possibilities in Sudan. The first possibility is the continuation of the present state of affairs. The government would continue to hang on and oppress the south until the situation gets bad enough that both internal and external reactions take place, resulting in the breakup of Sudan. Such a situation, however, involves many steps before finally arriving at the end result. The Sudanese People's Liberation Movement (SPLM) is itself broken up. The Sudanese continue to wrestle with the idea of whether they want a separate state or whether they want to be accepted as Sudanese.

The other possibility is the government's continued alienation of its own population by concentrating power and benefits within an increasingly narrow group, until finally it attracts so much external pressure that it is overthrown. That is what has happened to all preceding Sudanese governments. So far, the present government has taken care of those who would overthrow it and added its own ideological twist. Though being overthrown in this case may not be imminent, it is nevertheless an eventuality. What usually happens in Sudan is that the successor, in trying to address the problem with some kind of reconciliation between the north and south, is in turn overthrown by a hard-line government. On the optimistic side, overthrow might bring in a successor who is able to deal with the southern Sudanese problem. I think the southern Sudanese would be quite willing to deal with that possibility.

QUESTION: You said that one of the steps to resolving or helping collapsed states was external intervention coming in and leaving as soon as possible. Were you referring to international organizations and nongovernmental organizations (NGOs) as well?

MR. ZARTMAN: I was referring to the colonial phenomenon–the idea that either the United Nations or external states should be ready to get out as soon as possible. The problem that we are debating in connection with Haiti is a good example. There are no particularly limiting factors as to how long NGOs could remain. The problem of sovereignty is what leads me to say that foreign states should get out. NGOs do not have that problem and should continue to provide the support they can.

COMMENT: You did not mention the cases where deliberate attempts were made to cause collapse of a state, in most cases by religious fanatics. Examples of that situation are Nigeria, to some extent Egypt, and possibly even Sudan.

MR. ZARTMAN: These types of people do not want the collapse of a state. They want a portion of a state to collapse so they can assume power. My analysis rises above that situation. Groups like this may be ingredients in the collapse of the state. They may provoke the collapse of the existing state without being able to take over themselves. This is what happened in Algeria, where they contributed to the collapse of a state–not just a particular state, but the state as a function in Algeria. The state in Iran, by contrast, did not collapse. Instead, they replaced the state with a state of their own. Religious groups are a sign of the alienation of large parts of the population from the existing structure.

NARRATOR: We appreciate Mr. Zartman's time in making this presentation, as he is preparing to make an overseas trip, and thank him for adding to our knowledge of the countries of Africa.

CHAPTER THREE

Ethiopia: Yesterday and Today*

JOHN W. HARBESON

NARRATOR: John Harbeson's career exemplifies what many private foundations undertook to do in the 1960s. In the field of development, social scientists had a certain inferiority compared to representatives of the "hard sciences." The medical people and later the agriculture people went out into the field for long stints, while social scientists were accustomed to flying into an airport, giving a paper, and then flying out.

Professor Harbeson has had quite a different career. At a whole series of institutions he has not only gone to visit, he has gone to stay: Addis Ababa University in Ethiopia (1973-75), the University of Nairobi in Kenya (1965-67), and a whole host of other visits. He will be leaving almost momentarily for another regional assignment in east Africa.

Professor Harbeson has had a distinguished career at the University of Wisconsin and is now at City University of New York at the Graduate Center and the City College. He has been associated with the Land Tenure Center at Wisconsin and has taught at Johns Hopkins School of Advanced International Studies. For the next two years, he will be USAID's regional democracy and governance adviser for eastern and southern Africa, based in Nairobi, Kenya.

He has had an impressive publication record. He wrote an article in *Current History*, which frequently devotes issues to a single

**Presented in a Forum at the Miller Center of Public Affairs on 9 July 1993.*

region; this one happened to be on Africa. It was Professor Harbeson's thoughtful article that spurred my efforts to get in touch with him. We are delighted that he is here at the Miller Center.

MR. HARBESON: I was asked to talk about Ethiopia and its current situation, and I feel a little strange doing that, in part because my new assignment in east Africa will have me in Addis Ababa for the next two years. I will probably be able to give a much better talk after that experience than I can right now.

Ethiopia is one of the largest countries in Africa, with a population of well over 50 million at this point. It is a unique country in many ways–not least of which is the fact that it was, with the exception of what is now independent Eritrea, never colonized except for a brief occupation by the Italians during World War II. Ethiopia is also very much an African empire. The original Ethiopia–Ethiopia is shaped roughly like a big full-masted sailboat–was the northwestern quadrant of what is now Ethiopia. This was the ancient kingdom. At the turn of the century and beyond, through the endeavors of Emperor Menelik II, it expanded to roughly its present boundaries, which were maintained until a year or so ago when Eritrea became independent. Eritrea was tired of being a province and is now a country in its own right bordering the Red Sea, through which Ethiopia's main access to the Red Sea is located. The irony is that Ethiopia is an empire that has survived an age of decolonization.

In some of my writing, I have tried to make the case that Ethiopia is more than an empire, that if it were only an empire, it would have gone the way of other empires long since. There was a time in the early part of the 19th century when European colonialism was heating up, when for a variety of reasons the central government of Ethiopia had all but collapsed. It was just a figurehead that would not have been able to do much to protect Ethiopia from being sawed up or partitioned. Somehow Ethiopia managed to survive that 50- or 75-year period until the first of a series of energetic and enterprising modern emperors. There was also a period after World War I between roughly 1913 and 1930 when, for a variety of dynastic reasons, the same thing could have happened, and yet it did not. Again, around 1939-45, during World

War II, the same thing could have happened when the Italians occupied the country for a six-year period, forcing Emperor Haile Selassie into exile. The emperor's return could have been complicated; there are some recent publications detailing the extent to which, even then, the British in particular had an eye toward extending their then-fading empire.

So Ethiopia survived. I try to make the case in some of my writing that even though Ethiopia's structural framework was imperial in nature, some sense of nationhood or statehood grew up within that framework and survived, making possible at least in some sense the potential of a true nation-state in Ethiopia in the sense that we all understand it.

The point on which I will focus is the extent to which that embryonic and perhaps somewhat inchoate sense of nationhood has been severely tried and tested. Even as we speak, it is at a delicate stage when several things could happen–some of them good and some of them perhaps not so good.

I think the problem began under the last emperor of Ethiopia, Haile Selassie, whose reign spanned a 44-year period from 1930 to 1974. Many of us were first exposed to Selassie through his dramatic appearance before the League of Nations in which he appealed to the League to honor its collective security commitments and come to the aid of Ethiopia when it was being invaded by the Italians. Although the League of Nations did not respond, I think that internationally Haile Selassie took on a certain larger-than-life character.

During Haile Selassie's reign, the fault lines and the fissures that have impeded the possibility of the enduring nation-state of Ethiopia first appeared. It is my sense that despite the many admirable qualities of the emperor, some of his other qualities helped weaken what might or may still yet be an Ethiopian nation-state.

The just-deposed military regime of Mengistu Haile-Mariam, which lasted from 1974 to 1991, extinguished a genuine Ethiopian revolution, despite the promise of what was supposed to have been. It is my contention–and some of my colleagues disagree–that this revolution never really became a revolution. Indeed, some people say it was stolen, which is why the potentially progressive and strengthening initiatives that might have come to fruition did not, and the embryonic Ethiopian nation-state was further weakened. As a result, for the last two years, a successor regime has been trying to hold the nation-state together despite the loss of Eritrea and other regional tensions that could lead to the balkanization of Ethiopia. At the same time, the country is under intense international pressure to democratize and to embrace the private market sector. Thus, it is a regime attempting to consolidate itself, trying to preserve a sense of Ethiopian identity while at the same time responding to insistent pressures for economic reform toward privatization and political reform toward democratization.

What happened during Haile Selassie's regime that prepared the ground for Ethiopia's present political crisis? The emperor was gifted in the sense that he was a master of the old game of divide and conquer. He had a capacity to manipulate regional leaders and lords in their struggle for power, to play them off against one another in a way that preserved the emperor's power and collectively weakened theirs. He also had a capacity to co-opt a whole generation of Ethiopians who went abroad for education and studied at Haile Selassie's first university. These students were well aware of Ethiopia's increasingly anachronistic position as a traditional feudal empire (I think the word *feudal* is properly used) in a sea of political change across Africa and across the Third World. Still, many of them were successfully co-opted. There is a fine book written by my friend John Markakis that discusses this topic skillfully and really is *the* work on the subject.

In that sense Haile Selassie managed to consolidate his regime and to co-opt an elite that might have been a problem for him. The short-run gain of regime consolidation, however, held long-run disadvantages because as Selassie aged and lost the capacity for personal rule, potential successors among the elite had all been undermined. Indeed, almost everyone in every group who might have been a successor was, in fact, co-opted and identified with that regime.

The pressures that led to Selassie's overthrow in 1973 and 1974 were brought about first by the famine in northern Ethiopia, which was badly managed and, in fact, denied by the regime. Another source of pressure was the system of land tenure, which protected him and supported his regime and the elites that he had co-opted, but which stood in the way of any kind of real development. When these boiled over, Selassie was forced from power in 1974. In a sense, then, the consolidation of his regime really took place at the expense of an Ethiopian state, because when he left there was no one in a position to succeed him.

The other thing Selassie did that has come to fruition relates to Eritrea, the area that was once a part of Ethiopia along the Red Sea, which has become independent within the last two years. That particular part of what was then Ethiopia experienced 75 years of Italian colonialism from 1875 to about World War II, making it the one exception in Ethiopia's history of being free from colonial rule. Eritrea, therefore, had a different history and direction from Ethiopia.

The Eritrea question was a serious one after World War II and one that was a major problem for the then-fledgling United Nations. What emerged was a delicate, but not entirely satisfactory, compromise in the creation of an Ethiopian federation; Eritrea would be federated in a loose sense with Ethiopia and have its own parliament and so forth. Haile Selassie undermined the entire project, however, quite literally using his powers of co-optation to buy out the Eritrean parliament, which then voted to end the federation and return Ethiopia to a unitary state. At this point, the movement for Eritrea's liberation was born, beginning a 30-year struggle that culminated in 1991 with its independence. During that period Haile Selassie refused to return to anything approaching a more federal state and set out to defeat that liberation movement by military means. Essentially, what had begun as a constitutional struggle became a national and personal struggle. Losses of lives and materials on both sides made reconciliation almost impossible by the time Selassie was overthrown in 1974. Eritrea and Selassie's efforts at co-optation therefore contributed to the weakening of the Ethiopian state.

Ethiopia was ruled for the past 17 years by a military regime led by one man, Mengistu Haile-Mariam, which deepened the problem. It is important to understand that in the first six or eight months of 1974, this was a genuine popular upsurge that one had to witness, as I fortunately did, to sense it. The lighted match was a proposal to raise the gasoline tax, which upset the cab drivers. In turn, as rural groups began campaigning for real change, there was a growing sense of that this country was in the throes of revolution with no government in charge. Haile Selassie's efforts to control the situation proved ineffectual. The problem was that this movement for change was leaderless. Compounding the problem, the Soviets were then sitting in Somalia. For this reason, and because part of Ethiopia is ethnically Somali, the Ethiopian military was concerned about how the situation might evolve. Somalia had in the past expressed interest in bringing all Somalis, including those in Ethiopia and Kenya, under one roof and making one Somali state. Ethiopia's external vulnerability was therefore great. Hence, in Ethiopia there formed a military committee that proceeded to enact what one of my British BBC friends called a creeping coup–gradually arresting junior and more senior officers, gradually taking charge of this movement for change. One could tell early on that eventually the coup would reach the emperor, as it did.

Regarding this point, I think there was a general acceptance of the military's assertion of leadership. As soon as Haile Selassie was toppled in September 1974, however, the real problems began. The expectation was that this military regime would be transitional, it would turn power over to a civilian government, and implicitly, a democratic government would immediately emerge. The military position, however, was ostensibly that this occurrence would be suicidal. Without the necessary social and economic foundations, and with the kind of European-style feudal economic structure that supported Selassie's reign still in place, such a democracy would have decapitated the old regime, but the body of the old regime would have still survived. A real change could only take place if that social-economic structure were transformed, after which there could be civilian rule.

This was the manner in which the debate was framed. But the military regime, to its credit, enacted land reforms–particularly rural, but also urban land reforms–designed to really transform the land-based power of the traditional Ethiopian order. These reforms were very popular reforms at their inception. These reforms notwithstanding, the regime insisted that there was this tug of war between those who wanted to return to civilian rule right away and the military regime that wanted to continue until the reform process was complete.

The other part of the problem was that having removed all of the institutions of the old order and all of the old elites at the local and regional level, the military regime really had no structure of its own to put in place. It was a military regime sitting on top of a society in change and with no instruments of its own to maintain any kind of order. Thus, when it moved to maintain order, even while it allowed these changes to take place, it found itself often siding with the *ancien regime*. This situation convinced those who had wanted change in the first place that the military regime was really just another imperial regime, only of a different stripe. It was Haile Selassie's regime flying different colors, but basically unchanged. The situation at that time was posed as a struggle between order and change, and the military regime chose to pursue consolidation of its own position in a desperate effort to create legitimacy through the reforms. The military postponed the transition to civilian rule, which eventually alienated almost all of its civilian supporters.

At the same time the Eritrea situation remained unresolved. There was one brief moment in 1975, when the presence of the transitional leader, Aman Mikael Andom, who happened to be Eritrean himself, might have provided a chance to achieve some kind of rapport or settlement with the Eritrean liberation movement. That movement, however, was lost with the overthrow and execution of Aman along with 60 other figures of the old order. As a result, the Mengistu regime turned to a military solution in its conduct with Eritrea, which essentially became self-defeating, and thus the war became intensified. The military regime's struggle to maintain order and to reassert and consolidate its position for the purpose of preventing the breakup of the Ethiopian state became self-denying, because in the process it undermined the legitimacy of the reforms it had undertaken. This was the state of affairs throughout the 1980s.

The eventual goal of civilian rule, however, was never forgotten. A political party called the Workers' Party of Ethiopia was created, resulting in a nominal transition from a military regime to the Workers' Party, but in reality—and it fooled no one—it was really a military creation with a superficial dressing, which reminded people very much of what Haile Selassie did in the name of democracy during his time. It was very much like the situation in Nigeria, where the candidates and the party structure were created by military leaders. What legitimacy does such a government have?

This deepening shuffle over what the Ethiopian state really was led ultimately to the overthrow of the Mengistu regime in 1991, spurred primarily by the Eritrean movement. The Eritrean movement had made alliances with others, particularly to the south, and two parallel processes emerged: the Eritrean movement in the north and a Tigrean movement just south of Eritrea, which together led to the overthrow of Mengistu in 1991.

Presently, Ethiopia faces four or five crucial issues. There is an immense humanitarian crisis–famines and so forth–recurring. Ethiopia is still one of the three or four poorest countries in the world by all of the available measures. On that foundation, such as it is, there is the need for some regime to survive long enough to be able to craft a transition to some sort of constitutional democratic order. At the same time, the country is also under intense pressure to break up the socialized structures and the socialized economy that the military regime established. All of these factors are pressing on Ethiopia all at once, and it is precarious. Local and regional elections were held approximately a year ago and were observed by a team of international monitors. These monitors gave it middle marks on the low side, so the election process did not have the impetus that it should have had. It should have been a legitimizing movement, but it was not.

In addition, there are the problems of the new regime, which the Tigrean-based regime just south of Eritrea put together as a kind of multiethnic coalition to effect this change. I think it is fair to say that it has put the consolidation of its own power ahead of state building. The new regime has organized its own separate political movements in the areas where the other coalition ethnic groups are; it seems to be competing with its own former allies. That little tactic has resulted in the alienation of many of the peoples of the southern region, who are known as the Oromo, in addition to the fragmentation of its own coalition and an increase in the number of factions within the coalition.

At this point, I think it is fair to say that the future of the Ethiopian state is in question, not only in terms of whether there will be democracy or a private sector but also of whether there will be an Ethiopian state at all. What has happened to Eritrea may be replicated and we might see many states or statelets in that region. It has a capacity to become balkanized in the way that Yugoslavia has been. I do not want to sound too dramatic, but the potential is there. This possibility has been avoided at several points over the last 150 years, but there is no guarantee that Ethiopia will survive.

I leave you with this unanswered question because that is the way the reality is. The future of Ethiopia is very much hanging in the balance.

NARRATOR: Many of my generation remember the nobility of Haile Selassie when he appeared before the League of Nations in 1935 and Selassie's subsequent chapters, which you have described. As I thought about them, I remembered Arnold Toynbee's idea that for the most part, leaders perform and succeed in one function. They come along at a given moment in history; they are confronted by a problem that suits their skills, and they make their contribution to history. But then they either fail or leave the scene, or the world spotlight moves on to other interests. One wonders if this was the case with Haile Selassie. A mutual friend–the former president of the University and now a World Bank official–used to say that he doubted if Mengistu had read more than three lines of Marx, yet he came to power as a Marxist-Leninist leader. I have wondered if the story of Mengistu is in a way the story of someone who is neither a particularly potent ideological leader nor a skillful politician, because in the last days of his regime he suddenly reversed himself and began to bargain with the United States and others for aid, although he did not fool anyone. He may have gotten some aid, but there was too much skepticism about what he was up to and why he had not made such a move earlier. He was a rather pathetic figure in that last stage. In both of these cases one wonders about the historic moments of leadership.

Lastly, is it fairly well-documented that in the latter days of the Selassie regime an Eritrea solution of some sort might have been within reach? What might it have looked like?

MR. HARBESON: To answer the last question first, my sense is that probably, at least through the 1960s, there might have been a chance for a reconciliation. This is true in part because at that point the Eritrea movement was divided and went through a transformation that I have not previously mentioned. If there were a solution, it would have been a move back toward the status quo to some sort of federal solution, such as one backed by the United Nations. My contention is that in the 1950s before Haile Selassie's designs became clear, there was little serious opposition to that solution. The Eritrean movement began when that deal was broken. I'm not sure it is documented, but I think there is consensus among most of us that there was a chance, the last of which was in 1975 during the transition period.

On the question of Mengistu and Marxism, I think there were people around him who were true ideologues, but he was not. There is a certain parallel to Stalin. I have not talked about the then-Soviet Union's support for Mengistu, which was more tentative and skeptical than people realize. Mengistu was very much a Stalinist figure in that Stalin was no ideologue either, but he was a master of manipulation.

The observation you made about leaders and their moments in history is interesting. I think Haile Selassie had his moment at the League of Nations and maybe even into the postwar period. He was restored to his throne and did succeed in foiling British aims in Ethiopia during the late colonial period, but I think his moment passed. Some people have said that if he had lived to 70 instead of 85 and had left the throne to a successor in the early 1960s, he might be remembered differently.

A follow-up of that observation is related to the current crisis in Ethiopia. If leadership is a function of personality in crisis, the situation in Ethiopia is one in which there is certainly a crisis but there is no personality. Ethiopia may be waiting for the person of the moment to emerge.

QUESTION: I have three questions. First, is it possible to see the developments from February to June 1974 in terms of high politics inside the government circle, rather than a popular revolution outside the regime? Was it, in other words, a counterrevolution by the traditional Amhara aristocracy to reassert their positions vis-à-vis the central state created by Haile Selassie?

Second, Christopher Clapham is much more enthusiastic about the Workers' Party and the process of civilianizing the regime. He hints at the role of the Oromo in the military and in the Workers' Party establishment. I wondered what has happened to the Oromo presence in the regime since the 1991 takeover of the Tigreans?

Finally, what went wrong with Mengistu? If you take a Clapham-like view of the mid-1980s, Mengistu is singularly successful. He basically reproduces the political strategy of Menelik II in the late 19th century, using external resources to build up the new Ethiopian regime. Why does all this unravel so quickly in the 1980s?

MR. HARBESON: The period between February 1974, when Haile Selassie's cabinet resigned (which in Ethiopia was a profound and unprecedented moment in itself), to September, when he was finally overthrown, was an intriguing time. Was there a conservative countercoup in the making there? I think the answer is yes. You have to recognize that to some degree Haile Selassie had distanced himself from people–but mostly from Amhara, who thought that even Haile Selassie's brand of modernization was superficial. Selassie was identified with things modern from the start: He flew an airplane before they were safe, he encouraged education in Ethiopia, and he gave the grounds for the university. Even though Selassie has to be given only limited credit in this regard, this was more modernization than some of the traditional Amhara elite wanted.

For the last 13 or so years of his regime, Selassie had a commoner, a nonaristocrat, as prime minister. It is clear that when the regime was falling apart during this process of transition, traditional elites made an effort to grab power but were unsuccessful in doing so, prompting a military response. The effort was clearly there, but ultimately it proved unsuccessful.

What happened to the Oromo? The leadership of the movement to overthrow the regime came from the Tigreans. Tigre is the area just below Eritrea in the north. For military and political reasons, the Eritreans made alliances with Amhara groups but also with the Oromo to the south, who were brought into the empire by Menelik's conquest. Thus, it became a kind of multiethnic coalition and not any easy one, because the Oromo were suspicious of the Amhara and of the Tigreans because they had been colonized by them and had lost their lands in the south to these same people. It was a very tenuous coalition.

What has happened since 1991 is that in the process of regime consolidation, the Tigrean coalition, led by a man named Mella Zenawi, reached out to the Oromo People's Democratic Organization, which was created and supported by the Tigreans in opposition to the Oromo Liberation Front and has been the main liberation movement. The organization has been playing a kind of divide-and-conquer politics and is doing the same thing in other areas; thus, in a sense it has been fracturing its own fragile coalition rather than working with it. That action prompted the Oromo to opt out of the coalition and to boycott the elections last summer.

Your third question was about Christopher Clapham. Clapham has written a fine book on the Ethiopian revolution and I have learned a lot from it. We differ, however, on the question of whether it was a revolution to begin with. I am skeptical; he is less skeptical. My sense has been that Mengistu was never the clever general or politician that Menelik was, the emperor who put this empire together. Mengistu is more like an earlier emperor, Tewodros II, the first modern emperor in Ethiopia, who in the 1850s was a crusader for reform but whose reach exceeded his grasp. He was such a crusader that in the process of crusading, he undermined even his own friends. I think Mengistu is really closer to Tewodros than to Menelik.

QUESTION: Do you feel that the Eritrean independence sets a precedent not only for Ethiopia, but for the rest of Africa? In other words, is what you might call "politics from below" incapable of building the nation-state? If that is the case, do you see greater balkanization as a potentially new form of politics in Africa?

MR. HARBESON: I think that is yet to be determined. After African countries became independent in the early 1960s and then created the Organization for African Unity (OAU), all of the boundaries of the African states were accepted as previously and arbitrarily drawn. The OAU made the decision to accept those boundaries and work with them. That choice was the lesser of the two evils, and that position has been maintained to this day. Somalia was the only nation, as I hinted before, who never accepted that decision, and they have tried, at Ethiopia's and Kenya's expense, to change the boundaries to coincide with Somali spheres of influence.

Nevertheless, Eritrea is the only boundary change that has taken place in the 35 years of African independence, so it certainly sets a precedent. The possibilities for other such adjustments are very real. Whether these adjustments will extend elsewhere across the continent, I really do not know.

QUESTION: Your concern that Ethiopia may be the Yugoslavia of the future is accurate and is shared by many Ethiopians who live here. I think an immediate example could also be that of Somalia. In addition, rising Islamic fundamentalism is a problem in both Eritrea and Ethiopia.

I wonder how ethnic politics can be fused into party politics. I do not know any other African country where this merging has been possible. Do you think, for example, that the Tigrean preponderance is a pattern across centuries of Ethiopian history? Do you think it is a continuation of princely power based on ethnicity? Will U.S. involvement in setting the multiparty talks and discussions–it seems that only those with the military arms were present at the London conference–backfire? The near future could be very volatile. There are many Ethiopians who think that Mengistu's return might be an improvement, however cynical and sick that may be. Finally, how do you judge the longevity of the present regime, especially in light of the human rights violations documented by Amnesty International?

MR. HARBESON: Could Ethiopia be a Somalia? I think the potential is there, but it is a little different. My knowledge of Somalia is probably not as great as that of some people in this room, but Somalia strikes me as ironic because in some respects Somalia–in terms of culture, its almost universal adherence to

Islam, and its common language—has more of the ingredients necessary to build a nation than any other country in the continent, yet it is falling apart.

Ethiopia does not have that kind of cultural base. I have simplified greatly the degree of ethnic diversity. It is enormous, so Ethiopians do not even have that advantage.

In terms of ethnic politics and party politics, one of my concerns is that the movement for democratization is very much U.S.-led at this point. The U.S. model may not be the best one. In Belgium, the Flemish and the Walloons have managed for some time to work out a very successful power-sharing agreement. A scholar named Arend Lijphart has written with great eloquence about what he calls consociational democracy, a kind of decentralized democracy. Africa may be better served by drawing on European models rather than the U.S. model.

Ethiopian ethnicity has always been different from that of Kenya or other countries. It was based more on territory than on kinship, and the degree of ethnic solidarity was less definable and less rigid than in other countries. Also, a number of Oromo have embraced orthodox Christianity. It seems to me that what has happened over Ethiopian history is that there has been a kind of give-and-take, through intermarriage and the like, that Haile Selassie and his predecessors for all of their sins did understand. My sense is that redrawing the map of Ethiopia into ethnic compartments—this is Oromo, this is Amhara, and so forth—is very destructive because it treats Ethiopia like other African countries. It rigidly defines that which has happily not been quite so defined before. Thus, if you are a Tigrean, you draw attention to the fact that your base is only about 5 or 10 percent of the population. It seems to me that this changes the basis of ethnicity in a harmful way.

You mentioned fundamentalism. From what I understand, almost all of Islam in that part of the world is of the Sunni variety, and to this point, happily, it has not been the kind of Islamic fundamentalism one has seen in Egypt and elsewhere.

I do think that religious tolerance was one of the things Haile Selassie was fairly good at. He was known to give money for the building of mosques. He could live with the fact of Islam in

Ethiopia. Although he himself was a deeply religious orthodox Christian, there was a certain kind of easy tolerance in that country that I hope does not go away.

When it was clear that the Mengistu regime was going to fall, the United States did try to broker a succession. There was a conference in London with representation based on, as you said, who had the guns and who had the power in the Machiavellian sense with those who did not have guns or power being ignored, which in some ways should not be surprising. I do fault Secretary Cohen for anointing the EPRDF, the Eritrean movement, and saying Okay, you can go in and take Addis Ababa, which I think was a mistake. That was unfortunate, though I do not know how harmful it will be in the long run.

NARRATOR: A progressive movement occurred within the universities in Ethiopia which recognized that the university had to get out into the countryside. This was pursued at the beginning of the Mengistu regime but was traumatized by fears of lawlessness in the countryside, just as ministers were shot as they crossed the border. Was that movement doomed from the outset? Was it impossible for moderates like Aklilu, for instance, to have remained and spearheaded some of the movement to rural areas, making education more relevant to the needs of the people? Or was even Aklilu too closely tied to the *ancien regime* to pursue these reforms?

MR. HARBESON: In other words, could some of the people who had ties to the old order, and who were a part of the emperor's regime but nevertheless progressive, have been the basis for a different course? I guess we will never know, so it is safe to speculate. These people really were the point of contention. These are people I knew well and with whom I worked. Still, my crystal ball is very murky. If Haile Selassie had, perhaps, left the scene a few years earlier, this group would have inherited Ethiopia, and you might have gotten something a little different. I'm not sure the result in Eritrea would have been any different, but it is possible that you would have seen a more moderate regime. I'm not sure it would be ultimately democratic, but certainly it would have been more moderate and reformist.

One of the things that took place in the last ten years before all of this happened was something called the Ethiopian Universities Service. This was a requirement that all students at the university go out in the countryside for their third year and work among the people to improve such things as literacy, demonstrating that even though they were a favored elite, there was an obligation to the remainder of Ethiopia. It might have worked. Whatever would have happened, it would have been less unfortunate than what transpired.

NARRATOR: Many have commented on the clarity and intelligence of John Harbeson's writing. Even if one is not an expert in the field, what he is saying is always clear. That same quality has been demonstrated in his discourse. We are very grateful to him for this insightful presentation.

CHAPTER FOUR

The United States, the United Nations, and Somalia*

ADMIRAL JONATHAN T. HOWE

NARRATOR: Admiral Jonathan Howe, who is retired from the U.S. Navy, was, as a civilian, the special representative of the United Nations for Somalia from March 1993 to March 1994. Few people know about the large number of credentials he brought to this task. He received his bachelor's degree from the U.S. Naval Academy and his master's and doctoral degrees from the Fletcher School of Law and Diplomacy. For four-and-a-half years he served on the staff of the National Security Council (NSC) as assistant to National Security Adviser Henry Kissinger. He subsequently served as assistant for national security affairs to Vice President Nelson Rockefeller from 1975 to 1977.

His assignments in the Navy include serving as commander of a guided missile destroyer and as engineering officer of a nuclear submarine. He was commander of Destroyer Squadron Thirty-one, after which he became assistant secretary of state for politico-military affairs, serving under both Secretary Haig and Secretary Shultz from 1982 to 1984. As commander of Cruiser Destroyer Group Three and Carrier Battle Group Foxtrot from 1984 to 1986, he was responsible for conducting major operations and exercises in the western Pacific and Indian Oceans. He then served as deputy chairman of the NATO Military Committee in Brussels, Belgium, and as assistant to the chairman of the Joint Chiefs of Staff,

**Presented in a Forum at the Miller Center of Public Affairs on 1 August 1994.*

Admiral William Crowe. As commander of NATO's Allied Forces in southern Europe and serving concurrently as commander of U.S. Naval Forces in Europe and the Eastern Atlantic, Admiral Howe dealt with problems related to the Gulf War and many other crises. In late 1991 he became deputy assistant to the president for national security affairs, advising National Security Adviser Brent Scowcroft and President Bush on foreign, defense, and international economic issues.

Prior to assuming his U.N. duties, Admiral Howe was a consultant for national security affairs in the Bush-to-Clinton transition. We are delighted that he could be with us.

ADMIRAL HOWE: In a sense, Somalia is especially well-suited to be discussed as a presidential problem, in that it occurred during the transition from one administration to another. As Secretary Eagleburger knows so well, it posed particularly difficult problems for American foreign policy. I would like to discuss both the American and the U.N. experience with Somalia and what that experience has meant. Quite honestly, one must be working inside the United Nations to truly understand both its potential and its limitations. I will be speaking more from a U.N. perspective than a U.S. perspective because not many Americans have had that type of experience.

Somalia is important not just in its own terms, but because it affects what I would call the third tier of problems that the United States faces as a world leader; certainly the United Nation faces these problems as well. Americans sometimes forget that our country still has strategic responsibilities such as those associated with nuclear deterrence and proliferation and other "first tier" issues. There is also a second tier consisting of regional conflicts. For example, although there was divided opinion about U.S. involvement in the Iraq war, that crisis fits the traditional pattern of defining the national interest–countering an invasion, securing vital resources, and protecting a longtime friend. That was a regional conflict in which American power was used in a very traditional way.

This third tier of problems is hard for any administration and certainly for the United Nations to confront: genocide, ethnic cleansing, and starvation, all of which are man-made problems. Specifically, Rwanda, Somalia, Bosnia, and to some extent Haiti fit into this tier. There are no set, easy rules of thumb to follow in these situations and no risk-free solutions to the particular problems that are generated. They simply have to be confronted and addressed.

In discussing Somalia as an example of this third tier of world problems with which the United States is wrestling, it is important to distinguish fact from fiction–what happened, and what did not happen. Somalia is currently being used as an excuse for inaction, having become synonymous now with American foreign policy disasters and U.N. debacles.

The United States picked a real "lulu" when it chose Somalia as the first place to try to rebuild a failed nation. In other words, it was not traditional U.N. peacekeeping between sovereign countries, but peace*making* within a complex society. The United Nations was not mediating an international conflict, but it was moving into a country to stabilize it and to deal with a humanitarian disaster that had been created by men's greed and lust for power. The United Nations was trying to restore order in a country whose government, institutions, and supporting infrastructure (schools, water, electricity, police, and so forth) had collapsed. It did not have a self-sustaining economy and had not had one for 20 years. Somalia had been supported primarily by Russian aid and later by American aid; it was never 100 percent self-sufficient.

One of the most difficult problems has been that Somalia is a very clannish country. The Somali people's loyalty to their clans, subclans, and so forth makes it difficult to bring a sense of nationhood into that country. This is especially true in the wake of a civil war, which exacerbated insecurities. In the background, there was also a latent tendency toward fundamentalism by some groups–more properly called extremism–encouraged by interference from outside powers. Another factor that made this situation difficult was that the warlords–the faction leaders–were not exhausted from the fighting and were still seeking to gain power through military means. As such, the country was awash with weapons, and it still is.

From early December 1992 until March 1993, the United States was in the lead in Somalia. With the passage of Resolution 814 in late March, the United Nations began to assume overall responsibility, although the United States was still responsible militarily, during the subsequent ambiguous period. On 4 May 1993 the United Nations formally took over military security responsibilities as well. Some U.S. forces remained, however, until 31 March 1994.

The question of why the Bush administration decided to move troops into Somalia in December 1992 is important. It was an unprecedented decision for an American leader to make. It was not made because of strategic interests, although the United States is still accused of that in Somalia even today. With the demise of the Cold War, there was no strategic threat to the Horn of Africa; the Russians had left and the United States had left.

Traditional ways of resolving factional disputes already had been tried and exhausted in Somalia. Negotiators had tried and failed, and 50 U.N. military observers had been sent as well but were soon forced to leave. The U.S. Air Force launched an airlift to distribute food to the countryside where people were dying of starvation and to circumvent the obstacles in the port of Mogadishu. Other countries became involved in attempting to solve the problem of food distribution, but the civil war severely disrupted these efforts. A decision was then made to send 3,500 U.N. military personnel as "food guards" to help deal with food distribution from Somali ports. To expedite the process, the United States flew the initial U.N. contingent, 500 to 600 Pakistani soldiers, to Mogadishu airport. The situation was very touchy. A warlord named Mohamed Aideed and his SNA (Somali National Alliance) prevented them from ever arriving at the seaport to safeguard food shipments. The Pakistanis were frustrated because they were operating under Chapter Six of the U.N. Charter and did not have the authority or the power to move at will. Permission was required for them to travel in Somalia.

The United States became militarily involved because thousands of innocent people had been robbed of food relief shipments that had been sent in to feed them and conventional approaches in solving the problem had failed. In 1992, an estimated

300,000 people had died from starvation and disease in Somalia, including half of all children under the age of five. Predictions were that one-and-a-half million Somalis would die in 1993.

On the day before Thanksgiving day in 1992, Secretary Eagleburger was sent to talk to Secretary-General Boutros Boutros-Ghali about American willingness to lead a force into Somalia. Although the United States was willing to take a leadership role, there were conditions for its participation. First of all, the United States wanted other countries to help militarily in this endeavor. It did not want to have to deal with the problem by itself. Second, the United States insisted on having *peacemaking* authority, which came under Chapter Seven of the U.N. Charter. Force could then be used if necessary to carry out the food distribution mission. Third, the United States insisted that the mission be limited in time and narrow in scope, with no attempt at disarmament and a provision that the mission be turned over to a conventional U.N. peacekeeping effort as soon as possible. The resolution that subsequently was passed by the Security Council on 3 December authorized the use of: "All necessary means" (which means a great deal of flexibility to use force if needed) to provide a secure environment for the delivery of humanitarian relief.

There were major differences between having U.S. military leadership in Somalia and the subsequent U.N. leadership. As a superpower the United States was the dominant force in Somalia, with more than 20,000 troops on the ground backed by air, naval, and logistics capability. In contrast, when the United Nations assumed leadership on 4 May 1993, the largest contingent was 4,000 Pakistanis. With military units of many nations patched together, the U.N. organization was weak. In addition, the United Nations was given a much broader mission than the United States, and the United Nations was asked to carry it out throughout the country.

On 26 March 1993, the U.N. Security Council passed Resolution 814, the so-called nation-building resolution. It was hoped the resolution would give Somalia a chance for rebirth and to help establish a more lasting solution to the problems that had caused starvation and disease. As one of the principal architects of this resolution, the new United States administration felt this broad mandate was the right thing to do for Somalia at the time.

The United Nations planned to help Somalia's political, economic, and security recovery. Under the Addis Ababa Accords, to which the faction leaders had agreed shortly after Resolution 814 was passed, there was to be a two-year transition period in which district, regional and transitional councils would govern–followed, in due time, by a democratically elected government. Plans were also proposed to stimulate the agrarian economy toward self-sustaining growth by helping people find jobs and regenerating exports. Clearly, the reconstruction and development process would be long term. The rebuilding task was enormous.

The other U.N. objective was to transfer responsibility for security into Somali hands–to restore the police force and to get the judicial and penal systems working, which have to go hand-in-hand. Every Somali policeman on the streets meant a U.N. soldier could eventually leave. The sooner Somalis rather than U.N. soldiers were enforcing law and order the better. Even though the Addis Ababa Accords set a 45-day schedule for disarming the whole country, we knew that disarmament could not be done in the near term. Our objective was to get to the point within two years, perhaps, where the official Somali police would have better weapons than all of the bandits and militia running around in the countryside.

We got into difficulty on 5 June when the Pakistanis were viciously attacked by Aideed's SNA forces, and there were disruptions throughout Mogadishu. After that the man on the street, not only in the United States but throughout the world, thinks that U.N. forces spent all of their time chasing Aideed who was assumed to have orchestrated the assault. First, the United Nations did not have the means to do that. It was only after the U.S. Rangers arrived in late August that there was a trained capability to make an arrest while minimizing casualties on both sides. Second, we never opted for that strategy alone because it always seemed problematic. We never put faith in such a shortcut solution to the problem of Somalia. What the United Nations wanted to do was to continue on with the strategy that had been designed to try to help the whole country recover. Sporadic incidents in the ensuing months were mainly centered in south Mogadishu. During that time the United Nations pushed for political, economic, and security recovery. For example, 53 district councils were inaugurated under the terms of the Addis Ababa Accords–the beginning of real self-government in Somalia. District councils led to regional councils, which ultimately would form the basis for the transitional national councils. It took a tremendous amount of political work in the field, and work continued on schools, public health, water, electrical resources, and agriculture. The recovery of Somalia was what we were working on, not chasing Aideed. The U.N. strategy was to make progress in the rest of the country and to isolate Aideed within his political faction, the SNA. The SNA would be permitted to have a place in the transition government as specified by the Addis Ababa Accords, but Aideed could participate only if he answered the allegations against him through the courts. The U.N. belief was that the best way to isolate Aideed was to get on with the process of national recovery throughout the whole country. This was difficult to achieve, however, because civilian personnel, resources, and military forces were not provided in a timely fashion.

From the U.N. perspective, the experience in Somalia revealed many limitations. The United Nations is a dependent organization. It depends on the Security Council for guidance, and it depends on member nations to contribute military forces and to provide funds.

The United Nations in New York is not really streamlined; it is not geared up yet for this type of complex challenge. It is the ultimate in bureaucracies. The organization has many problems with which those of you who have worked in government are familiar, multiplied by about 100 times.

In the field, this translated into a severe lack of personnel. In the few last days I had before departing for my assignment in Somalia, my highest priority was to convince good people to go with me–talented, experienced managers who would follow through and get things done. The undertaking ahead of us was gigantic. In fact, I did not realize just how enormous it would be, but I knew we clearly needed many more people than we were able to recruit. When I arrived in Somalia in the middle of March 1993, UNOSOM I (United Nations Operation in Somalia) was only about half manned for its limited tasks. At the time I was basically watching what the Americans were doing during what was called the

UNITAF period. (The Unified Task Force was the name of the U.S.-led coalition in Somalia.) No one had looked at the anticipated personnel requirements that would come from Resolution 814. This broad mandate called for disarmament and demining, managing political recovery, economic development planning, reconstituting police and justice systems, media efforts throughout the country, and other challenging tasks. These jobs were very difficult. Several months later, after major efforts to obtain civilian assistance, my staff had only about 40 professionals, about 30 field service or administrative people, and some 60 technicians—communicators, guards, and so forth. That was it for the entire country! There was one telephone on my desk and that was all we had initially. My secretary did not even have a telephone. These are just illustrative examples of the problems of getting enough people organized for a civilian job in Somalia.

Lack of resources was another huge problem. A great deal of money had been assessed for the peacekeeping budget to support U.N. military forces, but we could not draw upon those funds for the things that we needed the most to make political, economic, and security efforts work. Humanitarian relief operations are usually funded by donations from nations. Nations had to donate money in addition to what they regularly gave to the United Nations and nongovernmental organizations (NGOs) for humanitarian relief. But we only got about 10 percent of the pledges that countries had made at a conference in Addis Ababa in March. The money did not come through, and as a result, we were not doing the job of assisting recovery to the extent that we could. Giving hope to the Somali people in the face of anti-United Nations propaganda from Aideed thus became even harder to do. Those of us who led the United Nations operation felt that we needed flexible funding. It took almost a year before we received money that we could use with greater discretion.

In order to fund the police and justice system, we had to spend more time begging—and so did U.N. officials in New York. By the way, Undersecretary General Koffi Annan, who is in charge of peacekeeping, and Elizabeth Lindenmeyer, who is the senior officer working in Somalia full time, are absolutely fantastic. The United Nations needs about 100 more of them to deal with a problem like

Somalia, however. They worked their hearts out to try to convince nations to give money to the police, justice and penal system. Unfortunately, it took a year of hard work and hundreds of meetings before that money came through. There are many other examples of how lack of resources frustrated our efforts to help the Somalis recover.

The multinational military presented a different set of problems. I have had several jobs in NATO, and I thought trying to convince 16 nations of something was hard. The United Nations is nothing like NATO! NATO looks like a streamlined and efficient organization compared to the United Nations.

This U.N. operation was not like Desert Storm. There was no dominant nation such as the United States with 500,000 troops and all of the exotic weaponry. We were dealing with an ambiguous situation with a patchwork quilt of small units from 20 (eventually 30) nations hastily knit together. The problem was that these nations individually put limits on what kinds of actions their forces would take or where they would serve. Thus, we were faced with a dilemma. We were desperate for manpower, so we had to accept these onerous conditions set by nations for joining the coalition. Another problem was that every nation wanted to micromanage its own forces, and they demanded the right to veto missions they did not like. Some troops stopped fighting in the middle of battles they could have won because they were called off by interference from a capital thousands of miles away. A military organization cannot be very good without unity of command or the ability to use what force it has in an emergency. Military training, equipment, and the ability of many of the U.N. units were simply not comparable to that of the United States. When the 20,000 American troops left, the U.N. troops that eventually replaced them were not nearly as capable. Multinational coalitions must also overcome the problem of language barriers and equipment interoperability.

Understandably, the Achilles heel was that nations do not want to pay the price in casualties. When lives are lost, it really focuses the policy dimension in terms of, Is this worth it? Are we going to continue to pursue this particular goal, or not? Some nations had little political tolerance for casualties. This was not a defense of their interests or national security; it was a mission of mercy to a failed nation. Putting together the military component turned out to be one of the most difficult aspects of building an organization that would work. By the way, the Somalia operation was supported logistically by civilian contractors. When the bullets start flying, are the civilian contractors going to continue to deliver, or are they going to say that their contract does not say they have to stay? This is a question that is not fully answered yet.

When people talk about lessons for the United Nations from this particular situation, I think they need to realize that the United Nations has many flaws that need to be fixed. Still, if U.N. forces are attacked and they just duck and look the other way, the United Nations will quickly lose effectiveness in that country, and ramifications ultimately will be felt by U.N. organizations throughout the world. Clearly, the U.N. military function has to be strengthened considerably. Some problems can be fairly easily corrected, but others involve inherent difficulties. The biggest problem is that nations are always going to want to retain some control over their forces. That is going to be a very difficult problem to overcome with the United Nations or any other kind of multinational force. Another inherent problem is that the United Nations is an organization of 180 nations, and securing agreement of the majority of these nations to support U.N. operations properly can be a big obstacle to overcome.

I believe there are problems in the personnel area, in the resource area, and even in the military area that can and should be remedied to make the United Nations better. From the U.S. standpoint, an assessment of where the United States is going and what it is doing needs to be made at every important juncture. Before U.S. forces went into Somalia, the U.S. government may have overestimated the ability of the United Nations to pick up the ball with a peacekeeping force after U.S. forces left. I think the United States underestimated the degree of difficulty of decoupling itself from such a mission once it had begun.

Another lesson is that when Americans intervene somewhere, they have to make it work. In considering the original mission, it is important to determine whether or not the United States could just provide humanitarian relief as its original undertaking implied, or would it have to deal with the underlying political problem. In other words, would the United States and the United Nations treat the symptoms or cure the sickness? The United States needs to reassess the situation at each critical juncture. When Resolution 814 was passed, for example, its objectives were much broader than previous ones. The United States needed to ask, Are we still committed? What exactly are the objectives of this expanded mission? Are we willing to support them? Once the United States is committed, it should stick with the agreement and make it work. For example, the United Nations asked for a delay in the change of command from the United States to the United Nations from 4 May to 4 June because it did not believe it was ready, and the request should have been taken seriously. On 5 June the U.N. forces were attacked. Would there have been a difference if the United States had stayed until the fourth of June? Probably, but we do not know–it is all very speculative. The point is that later on when the United Nations was under attack and passed an emergency resolution asking for things, the United States was obliged to help make it work. The United States needed to think in terms of how to make the mission successful, not how to avoid dealing with it.

In conclusion, I think the United Nations will be a useful and vital instrument in the future, but it needs to be improved. I do not think genocide and ethnic cleansing can be tolerated. There are certain moral standards that virtually compel people to do something. The threat of force will have to be used sometimes, even if it is only to create the conditions for a negotiated solution, which, of course, is always preferable. No one wants to use actual force! Using force is a sign of failure to a certain extent in peacekeeping, but the United Nations needs to have it and be ready to use it if necessary.

The United States needs to be selective about what it engages in, but it should not be paralyzed by a "post-Somalia syndrome." Each case needs to be examined carefully. This country is very important to the success of the United Nations and to any collective response to these situations in which state authority collapses. The United States, however, must have achievable goals and it must persevere. The United Nations must also have sufficient means to carry out its missions. Resources, people, and the necessary force must be provided if relief workers get into difficulty.

I think most people want a world that is policed, but Americans do not want the United States to be the world's policeman. So, what can be done? With humanitarian issues we have to ask the question, When is intervention interfering with the rightful political processes within a country, and at what point does a situation become so repugnant to civilized people that something has to be done? Genocide or holocaust certainly qualifies as a basis for intervention in my mind. But the biggest question that Americans need to ask themselves is, Is there a broader national interest at stake? Is there a *world interest*, an interest shared with others, that would cause us to be willing to take the risk?

Finally, even though some people disparage the U.N. operation in Somalia, they should remember that thousands of lives were saved. The last chapter has not yet been written. There are still 19,000 U.N. troops and many courageous U.N. civilians there trying to help the Somali people. The future is now much more dependent upon the Somali faction leaders, however. We do not know whether the United Nations' investment in Somalia will be enduring or not, but the agonizing lessons learned as a result of the Somali experience, both for the United Nations and the United States, will endure and should be studied.

QUESTION: How would you evaluate the role of Ambassador Robert Oakley in terms of his personal diplomacy?

ADMIRAL HOWE: I personally worked with Ambassador Oakley for many years, and I feel that when President Clinton sent him back to help in Somalia, he had an instructive catalytic impact in moving the negotiations on to the next phase. In a sense it was an appeasement phase, or a nicer word would be a reconciliation phase. The only way that Somalia could retain the support of the United Nations was to bring the faction leaders together in reconciliation, and people have worked extremely hard to make that possible. The Oakley mission was helpful in that regard. Other people might have a different view, but I feel he is a very capable person.

COMMENT: The *Christian Science Monitor* recently had an editorial that fits in with your discussion. It called for the creation of a U.N. fire brigade; in other words, a stand-ready group of military men and civilians from countries that had already given them permission and had set the conditions under which they could go into a conflict situation. Such an arrangement would avoid the laborious negotiations that take place at the onset of every incident.

ADMIRAL HOWE: After my experience in Somalia, I would like to see something like that, but it should be tried carefully on a trial-and-error basis. A U.N. "foreign legion" is needed, a cadre of highly competent civilian and military people with national forces assigned to them. This plan would be useful for the future in that it avoids the problem of national interference. It would truly be a U.N. force, as opposed to country *X* dealing with a particular problem on behalf of the United Nations. It is an attractive possibility that needs a great deal of coordination and time to implement. I would be in favor of working in that direction, but meanwhile, we have to work more in terms of a large dominant force like the U.S.-led UNITAF. To function well in a dangerous military situation, the force should consist of large units from just a few nations that have agreed on the goals, instead of 30 nations, as in UNOSOM. Nations have to agree on the fundamental objectives before they go in.

QUESTION: Do you believe anything has changed in Somalia that will endure in the long term?

ADMIRAL HOWE: For the short term, thousands of hungry people are still alive. Long-term effects remain to be seen. Somalia is a complicated country and has been so for thousands of years. People are still working very hard to establish a transitional government and to move eventually into an elected system. Meanwhile, there is work going on throughout the country on the educational system, basic health, and other kinds of recovery projects.

We have all seen televised pictures of battles in south Mogadishu and of Somalis committing dreadful acts of violence. There are also many wonderful Somali people living at peace, unbeknownst to most Americans. The women are terrific–one day they may be regarded as the saviors of that nation. They work hard; they want peace; they are sick of war. They have to care for the orphans. Most of their husbands are either dead or lame. This country has many things going for it that are very reassuring. There is a religious movement that is well-meaning in its mission. So how is it all going to come out? That is hard to say. I telephoned someone who works on Somalia yesterday and asked how things were going. He told me which places were under attack, and overall he was pretty pessimistic. I think it is too soon to judge.

QUESTION: Is it reasonable to assume that tribalism and hunger will return?

ADMIRAL HOWE: I hope not, but my feeling was that if the United Nations had succumbed to the temptation to wrap up the operation and not stay the two years that was deemed necessary for Somalia to recover, disease, hunger, and chaos would have rapidly returned because the recovery was so fragile. It is possible they could go back to that situation. I hope not, but there is still too much fighting going on there.

SECRETARY EAGLEBURGER: I would like to comment because the last question raises a point about which I have been thinking. I do not think that American involvement entails a commitment to do something for Somalia over the long term. With regard to what the United Nations ought to be doing in the future, this administration and the United Nations ought to be spending a great deal more time considering the issues Admiral Howe has raised here today and begin to learn some lessons. Unfortunately, I do not think that is being done.

At the same time, people have to be very careful of what they are asking that institution to do, or if the United States acts unilaterally, what it is being asked to do. It seems to me that intervening in Somalia simply to save people from starvation was worth it. That does not mean that the outside world should take on the task of trying to solve the puzzle of that country's politics for the next ten years. The Somalia case convinced me that when these kinds of tragedies take place, there will be an irresistible clamor to do something. I could have told you a month ago that the United States would have to go into Rwanda. I think we waited much too long, and many people have died unnecessarily. U.S. intervention does not mean the United States can solve the longer-term problem of the relationship between the Hutus and the Tutsis, however. What it does mean is that some people can be kept alive and hopefully provided with some modest stability to permit the rebuilding of the nation.

The other issue to be considered is whether this can be accomplished at costs that the U.N. member-states are prepared to pay. I can tell you from personal experience that the Bush administration decided to intervene in Somalia because it knew it could be successful and that it was not going to cost thousands of dead and wounded American troops. Intervening in Yugoslavia would entail a much higher risk of casualties, even though the extent of human tragedy may be equal to that of Somalia. I can assure you that the last administration would never have done so. One of the things that we in the Bush administration certainly considered was whether trying to solve this case, as awful as it is, would cost much more than the American people were prepared to pay, therefore making it more difficult to take action when a similar situation with greater prospects for success arises in the future.

The tragedy of Somalia, in a way, is that we chose to "cut and run" when we lost some troops, and because of that decision, the United Nations got an undeservedly bad reputation in this country. Some people in my own political party have been playing games with this issue ever since, insisting that our country cannot send in troops unless they are under the command of the president, and so forth. We have learned some wrong lessons from the experience in Somalia. We have not sat down and thought hard about how the United Nations ought to function and what kinds of cases it should handle. These kinds of tragic cases are going to be with us for decades to come, and the United States must be careful and not take on more than it can handle.

Has the United States made a difference in Somalia? Perhaps not, but for the 250,000 people who once faced starvation and are still alive, that is a long-term difference for them. The United

States is going to have to do the same thing in Rwanda, and it will have to do it in a big way to save lives, although U.S. assistance does not mean the United States can solve longer-term problems. Overly ambitious intervention missions can get U.S. troops into a situation from whence the United States cannot easily extract them. Yet in spite of the risks, the United States must be ready to influence events in some cases.

QUESTION: I would like to ask Admiral Howe and Secretary Eagleburger whether anyone has ever given thought to the root cause of these conflicts and considered bringing to justice the Rwandan tribal leaders who have caused all of the suffering? According to recent reports, both parties are building up their strength once again. Those who have caused all of this trouble from the beginning should be brought to justice. What organization, if any, should handle this situation?

ADMIRAL HOWE: Those of us who led the U.N. operation in Somalia felt there should be some kind of fair and straightforward legal accountability. We had many debates over whether this requirement should be done in a single country or internationally. We spent a great deal of time discussing what should be done if General Aideed was ever arrested.

In Yugoslavia, there is an international crimes tribunal to which the United Nations have appointed international judges to try to deal with that problem.

SECRETARY EAGLEBURGER: That method will never succeed, by the way! We will never get a complete answer, although it would be nice if we could. In the first place, capturing these people is difficult, as you know from your experience with Aideed. I'm not against it; I just think it is highly unlikely in the Yugoslav case. Some of these criminals are the same people with whom the United Nations is now negotiating. We are stuck with them. In the case of Rwanda, I do not know how the people can be caught.

QUESTION: I understand there are some differences between the Somali experience and the Rwanda experience, but also some similarities. Is Nigeria next? If so, it would be a far larger-scale tragedy, and that would bring up the question Secretary Eagleburger raised: Given that it is a much larger country with a much larger military, could the United States successfully intervene?

ADMIRAL HOWE: On the continent of Africa, there may be three or four Somalias and Rwandas waiting to erupt, and they are all different. As Americans and as world leaders, we are going to have to come to grips with the question of what to do with those kinds of tragic circumstances. It is in vogue to say that preventive diplomacy is the answer. Of course, if you can do it, that's wonderful. I happen to agree with Secretary Eagleburger in the case of Rwanda, even though that crisis broke out suddenly in April–at least as far as the public was aware. Action could have perhaps been taken sooner, even though it was a tough situation. It would be nice if preventive diplomacy could stop these catastrophes from coming to fruition, but it is more likely that these problems will keep coming up. Try as we will to prevent them, they will hit us in the face, and we will just have to deal with very tragic humanitarian catastrophes in Africa and in other countries as well.

NARRATOR: You talked about the desirability of an international police force, and you mentioned Chapter Seven. What happens when we establish criteria of that kind for the first time? How do you make decisions about such questions when there is a total lack of means?

ADMIRAL HOWE: My recommended solution would emphasize the United States or other strong nations pulling together to help under the auspices of the United Nations, rather than leaning on a weak U.N. organization that does not have that capacity right now. If Americans feel that these needs are great enough and must be addressed, then we have to be willing to take the risk and go ahead and vote with our feet. Again, none of these situations are risk-free! Inevitably, some casualties will occur in places like Rwanda.

SECRETARY EAGLEBURGER: To me the tragedy is in not drawing lessons from cases like Somalia and thinking about what should be done to improve so that the next time such a crisis erupts, a more rational judgment can be made and an organization can begin to deal with it. If each time we are faced with such a challenge we throw something together at the last minute, it will always end up badly if it works at all, and we are going to make some very seriously wrong decisions. The tragedy of the Somalia case is that it has given the United Nations a rather bad name, which is totally undeserved. What we should all have been doing is drawing the lessons from that experience by putting together some form of international police force, if you want to call it that. There will be terrible trouble if people start arguing that U.S. forces should be under the command and control of some foreign authority rather than the U.S. president, and I do not believe the issue needs to go that far. I think the United States should be learning the lesson so that once it has put something together, a decision on a case-to-case basis can be made as to whether the United States should become involved. I would have to be dragged kicking and screaming into intervening in Nigeria because it would be another swamp, as I think Yugoslavia is. Rwanda and Somalia are the kinds of cases that probably can be handled, and we ought not apologize if we can deal with those cases but cannot deal with the more grandiose cases. For the next 20 to 30 years, I think more and more of these kinds of problems will be seen. That is what the world is going to be like, but people are not thinking hard enough about how to deal with it.

NARRATOR: We want to thank Admiral Howe and Secretary Eagleburger for an informative and wise exchange of ideas on this issue.

CHAPTER FIVE

Peacekeeping and Humanitarian Crises*

ROBERT B. OAKLEY

NARRATOR: Ambassador Robert Oakley retired in 1991 after serving 34 years in the foreign service. Secretary Eagleburger, who is responsible for our contacting Ambassador Oakley, said that he has never been unreservedly enthusiastic about the foreign service except when considering Bob Oakley, whom he places at the very top of the foreign service organization.

Mr. Oakley was born in Dallas, Texas, attended South Kent School in Connecticut, graduated in history and philosophy from Princeton University, and did graduate work at Tulane University before joining the foreign service in 1957. He has been ambassador to Somalia, Pakistan, and Zaire. He served twice in the National Security Council in senior positions, was director of the State Department Office of Combatting Terrorism, and was deputy to the assistant secretary of state for East Asian and Pacific affairs, Richard Holbrooke.

Mr. Oakley is a public servant of great distinction. We have all seen him in action on television recently when he was called back to Somalia after certain difficulties developed. In addition to such public service, he also has been associated in the private field with the Carnegie Endowment for International Peace and the United States Institute of Peace. Mr. Oakley's wife, Phyllis Oakley, likewise had a very distinguished career, returning to the foreign service

**Presented in a Forum at the Miller Center of Public Affairs on 15 September 1994.*

after a period of absence. She currently is the assistant secretary in the State Department's Bureau of Population, Refugees, and Migration. Mr. Oakley's topic today is certainly relevant on the eve of what may or may not be an invasion of Haiti.

MR. OAKLEY: Let me begin by briefly discussing the uncertain state in which we find the world today. Increasingly, we are seeing a phenomenon of anarchy and of failed states. Tremendous pressures are placed upon those societies without strong institutions, pressures in part brought on by the uncertainties of the world without the Cold War. The disappearance of the Cold War brought numerous factors that no one predicted. There was a psychological impact both on the strong countries, including our own, and on the smaller, weaker countries, as each was left to determine which way to go in the world. The loss of sponsorship made this impact particularly pronounced in the latter cases. These countries previously had either the United States or the Soviet Union behind them, and they had felt comfortable in that position. In some ways, it made them less vulnerable to popular protest and mass uprisings, although in some cases there was guerrilla warfare sponsored by one side in the Cold War against the other.

One must also note the pressures of population versus resources and other environmental concerns that impact the world today. To this list I would add the disconcerting, perhaps corrosive, and even destructive impact of modern communication. Everyone sees what is happening elsewhere, and they have a tendency to think that what is happening elsewhere is so much better than what they have at home. Therefore, they think they should do something about it. If they see someone staging a demonstration somewhere, they want to do likewise because it seems like the best way to get what they want. All of these factors have made for a great deal of uncertainty in what was supposed to be an orderly new world.

Somalia is a good case in point, and so is Liberia and more recently, Rwanda. In the former Soviet Union, Tadzhikistan and numerous other areas are unstable. The case of Somalia can teach us a number of lessons.

First, the international community has been very reluctant to become seriously involved in what are essentially internal problems.

At the same time, there are fewer barriers that would inhibit such involvement. International lawyers now argue that certain situations–concerning human rights, for example–should be interpreted as a potential threat to international peace and security. Human rights gives the international community justification for intervening in what used to be the sacred grounds of internal affairs covered by Article 27 of the United Nations Charter.

Perhaps because the Cold War is gone and people are no longer preoccupied with the threat of major conflicts, nuclear or otherwise, between the Warsaw Pact and NATO, they are able to pay more attention to problems of a different nature and magnitude. Perhaps because the veto in the Security Council is no longer being used since the Russians and Americans tend now to see things in the same way, the United Nations Security Council is being used more often. Security Council resolutions now average around 100 per year. I sometimes say they are turning out resolutions like sausages. This used to be the realm of the General Assembly, and this new level of activity for the Security Council changes the whole nature of the role it plays.

It also changes the basis for what is going on in the world. The United States has gotten justification from the Security Council to intervene in Haiti. The Russians have gotten Security Council endorsement to be the peacekeepers in Georgia's internal affairs. The French took action in Rwanda, and the United States took the initial action in Somalia. The latter was a somewhat different situation than either Desert Storm or the Korean War, the two previous times when the Security Council agreed to mandate an international operation led by the United States to deal with a security problem. There is now much more willingness, in theory, to intervene for the purpose of dealing with serious humanitarian, political, and security problems. In reality, however, a great deal of reluctance remains. For example, no one was willing to seriously intervene in Liberia. An envoy was sent to talk to them, but when that did not work, the West Africans had to take the matter into their own hands.

Little attention was paid to Somalia until Boutrous-Ghali became secretary-general of the United Nations. He had watched Somalia closely as Egypt's minister of state for foreign affairs, and as U.N. secretary-general he began to urge that some action be taken. At one point, he compared the international community's reaction to Bosnia and to Somalia, wondering if the disparity could be attributed to racism. The Security Council admitted that a problem existed but it still was not willing to go very far. Therefore, in April 1992 Boutrous-Ghali recommended an armed peacekeeping force of 500 people to protect humanitarian operations in Somalia.

At that time there was a cease-fire in effect, and Ambassador Sahnoun had just been sent as the secretary-general's special envoy. Boutrous-Ghali's efforts might have had some effect were it not for the Security Council's resistance, led by the United States. The Security Council was unwilling to get involved that deeply in Somalia's affairs. It would cost money, and the United Nations was already overburdened with too many other activities and operations around the world. Angola was a good example, and it was not going well. The Security Council therefore approved 50 unarmed monitors instead of Boutrous-Ghali's 500 armed peacekeepers–they agreed in principle that the 500 peacekeepers were acceptable but for the moment only sent the 50 unarmed monitors. When the monitors arrived, they were able to do absolutely nothing.

By the time the 500 armed peacekeepers had been explicitly approved by the Security Council and the necessary arrangements had been made, it was September 1992 and the situation in Somalia had deteriorated so badly that even these peacekeepers could do nothing. They could only sit in the port where they landed. Their mandate required them to obtain permission from the local authorities before taking any action, and they were weak in comparison with the warlords and faction leaders, particularly General Aideed, who were not about to allow them any real involvement.

All of America knew what was happening in Somalia, having seen it on television and read about it in the newspapers. There was tremendous pressure–particularly as a result of television coverage–on the United States to respond. Finally, President Bush, who had a strong humanitarian streak and believed in the United Nations, said that since no one else was willing to take action, the United States would.

The U.S. military had previously said that it wanted no part of the situation. Now that action was going to be taken, however, it had a plan for doing it right. Its plan was put on the table in the middle of November, and it called for two U.S. divisions. This proposal absolutely shocked planners in the State Department; they had been thinking in terms of a few hundred soldiers. If the United States were to take the lead in this international operation, however, two divisions were needed for maximum force. The military believed that this would minimize casualties among both the U.S. soldiers and Somalis. Going in with overwhelming force would be like putting out a small fire in the forest before it became a raging forest fire–it could be extinguished, but one had to act decisively and forcefully.

This peacekeeping force was offered to the United Nations, but it said that the plan was unacceptable because the United States wanted to be in charge, which was contrary to all of the traditions of peacekeeping. The operation therefore could not be a U.N. affair, but the Security Council could bless it. The United States agreed to do it that way and was soon joined by 23 other countries in sending peacekeeping forces to Somalia. It was a limited mission to protect humanitarian operations, and it was aided by over 60 nongovernmental organizations from around the world, plus the Red Cross, UNICEF, the World Food Program, the United Nations Development Program (UNDP), and a number of other international agencies. These organizations had previously been unable to do much due to heavy fighting taking place.

In addition to aiding the humanitarian operations, the United States also sought to create enough security for a traditional United Nations peacekeeping force to take the place of U.S. forces. For obvious reasons, that endeavor makes a great deal of sense politically. It also made sense financially, because as long as the United States remained in the lead, it would be paying the bill. When the operation became a United Nations concern, the U.S. share of the cost would go down to around 25 percent. The generals in charge of this operation and I found that we shared a determination not to get so deeply involved in Somalia's affairs that the United States would actually take over. Vietnam had taught us that lesson. In the long run, it is unacceptable to be running someone else's country–it generates a great deal of resentment. In the short run, one gets dragged into intractable dilemmas.

We were also determined to stay out of harm's way; that is, what was meant to be a pacifying operation would not slip, consciously or unconsciously, into taking sides in a domestic conflict. We watched that happen in 1983 in Lebanon. Traditional peacekeeping, as defined by Dag Hammarskjold and Ralph Johnson Bunche, was to remain neutral. In the case of Lebanon, the United States took sides. The initial deployment of the U.S. Marines was neutral, but with the second deployment it became very partisan. The United States did not quite understand what it had done and did not understand the local reaction, which was to see the U.S. soldiers as either allies or enemies. The outcome was the terrorist bombing of the Marine barracks. A considerable price was paid, and the United States was determined that it not happen again in Somalia.

At the same time, there was plenty of military force in Somalia, and the approach was to exercise maximum restraint in employing it. If attacked, retaliation would be hard and fast. These ground rules were well known because within 48 hours of our arrival we were broadcasting by radio in the Somali language. We had leaflets printed in Somalia that were widely distributed, and we set up a newspaper in Somalia that eventually reached a distribution of 20,000 copies. We were able to recruit some Somalis whom we knew from previous contact as well as some Somali-Americans, who aided in disseminating our version of what was happening. They made known our intentions and what was happening in the humanitarian field. Furthermore, we broadcast Islamic verses and prayers by radio to show that we were not anti-Islamic. This was all done to clearly establish both our intentions and the ground rules by which we would operate.

When these rules were violated in a way that was a direct threat to the Unified Task Force (UNITAF) forces, the response was quick and precise. This approach worked every time because we demonstrated strength on the ground, delivered humanitarian assistance successfully, and maintained neutrality.

When some of the more ambitious, unscrupulous leaders, such as my friend General Mohamed Farah Aideed, wanted to use force to extend their power and further their interests, we were able to prevent it. No one was allowed to use weapons for any purpose—

political or otherwise. We did not try to take the weapons away, however, because trying to disarm the whole country would be madness and would mean immediate conflict. Instead, weapons would be collected gradually as tensions subsided.

Different groups agreed to put their heavy weapons in various locations kept under surveillance by U.S. forces. Politically, we told them they were going to settle their own differences. We were not going to be the judge. We would, however, create a situation in which resolution would be possible in accord with their traditional ways of resolving disputes. We would ensure there was a safe place for them to gather and talk for as long as necessary. (We stopped serving food after a while because we found it prolonged the stay a bit too long.)

The Somalis did, in fact, set up the necessary mechanisms. Each side designated representatives, and fairly soon they organized themselves into two joint committees, one for humanitarian affairs and one for security matters. This structure for conflict resolution was replicated in the various centers around the country. Things were being done in the Somali way. We were not becoming too involved, but neither were we letting them fight it out. We encouraged them to resolve it through their elders, their religious leaders, or anyone else of their choice, as long as it was done peacefully. We also encouraged them to begin developing ideas for government, and at the end of March, they held a big meeting in Addis Ababa and arrived at a formula.

By then I had gone, and Admiral Jonathan Howe arrived just as the United Nations began to take over. On 4 May the United Nations took over militarily from the United States, and we left behind a residual battalion called a quick reaction force in support of the other military units present. The U.S. combat forces remaining in Somalia were under the command of the deputy U.N. forces commander, who is an American. The senior commander was a very good Turkish general.

During the transition from United States leadership to United Nations leadership, there was also a transition from the Bush administration to the Clinton administration. Compounded with this was a lack of clarity as to what precisely the United Nations was going to do when it assumed control in Somalia. The United

States did not insist upon clarifying this responsibility in part because this concern was lost in the shuffle between the two administrations and also because things appeared to be going reasonably well when the Clinton administration came into office. The United Nations, in effect, assumed that it could continue to rely on the United States to lead in Somalia, even if nominally it was the United Nations now in charge.

The new Clinton administration was enthusiastic about testing its new ideas concerning the rebuilding of failed states, assertive multilateral diplomacy, and more vigorous use of the United Nations. Somalia looked like a good testing ground, and a number of senior members of the United Nations, particularly the British, the French, and even the Russians, were intrigued by the idea. Secretary-General Boutrous-Ghali was certainly enthusiastic about it, as his agenda for peace included a much more active United Nations. Thus, the Security Council resolution that mandated the new U.N. operation in Somalia, taking over from the United States, was very far-reaching. The secretary-general's report to the Security Council, which served as the basis for the resolution, talked about disarming everyone, and it emphasized coercive rather than cooperative measures.

The United Nations took upon itself a broad mandate that became quite intrusive, and the United States supported it enthusiastically. Soon, the United States and the United Nations were interpreting what the Somalis themselves had agreed to in the conference in Addis Ababa, from which they further interpreted who were the good Somalis and who were the bad Somalis. They saw General Aideed and his Somali National Alliance (SNA) as disruptive to the desired outcome, based upon their interpretation of the Addis Ababa agreement, and they therefore sought to marginalize him politically. Aideed, however, refused to be marginalized.

In the eyes of the local people, the United Nations' role was becoming increasingly partisan, and many of them rejoiced because they did not like Aideed. The psychological impact of the situation's being handed over to the United Nations, however, had not been foreseen. Many Somalis expected things to fall apart when the U.S. forces left. We tried to explain that we had already reduced our forces considerably, that a substantial residual force would remain, and that the forces from the other contributing countries would remain as well. We also expressed our confidence in the Turkish lieutenant general who was assuming the senior command position.

Interestingly enough, the psychological effect was felt on both sides. The Somalis expected the U.N. forces to be weak and were determined to test them. The U.N. forces felt insecure, particularly the Pakistanis, who had assumed responsibility for southern Mogadishu. The Pakistanis' training and way of thinking were different from that of the U.S. Marine Corps. As a result, they disregarded the advice the Marines gave them before leaving.

The Pakistanis were told to continue two U.S. practices, both political and military in nature. First, they were told to maintain open dialogue with Aideed, military to military. The U.S. forces stayed in contact with him and the other Somali leaders every day, even when angry with them. Frequently, some of the more enlightened people in Aideed's camp would tell the U.S. forces when Aideed was receiving bad information or bad advice, giving the United States the opportunity to defuse some potential problems. This open dialogue kept the United States from being seen as the outright enemy.

Second, the Pakistanis were told to keep their patrols on the street day and night, just as the United States had done. All of the heavy weaponry and most of the militia had been pushed out of Mogadishu by constant U.S. patrols, and the militia had stayed out, knowing that U.S. forces would respond rapidly and resolutely if anything happened to their patrols. The Pakistanis, however, were neither trained for this duty nor felt comfortable with it (perhaps because they did not have tanks, which the U.S. Marines had had but did not use), so they stopped patrolling, particularly at night. Soon the militia and the weapons were back in the city.

Aideed, seizing the opportunity, decided to confront the United Nations rather than allow it to push him out of a political role in his country. He began to build up militarily, giving him the strength for a political challenge. Soon the United Nations decided to reassert itself and began inspecting weapons storage sites, one of which happened to be next door to Aideed's radio station.

There had been plans on the drawing board to seize the station because Aideed was broadcasting a great deal of anti-United Nations propaganda. The United Nations, including the U.S. commanders, did not properly appreciate that the radio station had become Aideed's *causus belli.* When they searched the radio station for hidden weapons, to Aideed's people, they had seized the station. They were actually only there for 30 minutes, but by the time they left, word of the station's supposed seizure had spread through town. When Pakistanis came out of the radio station they were ambushed, and over 20 Pakistani peacekeepers were killed. The United States and the United Nations responded by condemning this attack upon peacekeepers and declaring Aideed's organization to be the enemy.

Frustration continued to build in the ensuing months, as there was little success in stopping Aideed. On 12 July, U.S. helicopter gun ships launched a surprise attack on a compound where most of Aideed's SNA leadership was meeting. Some elders from the Habergidir clan happened to be present, as well as people from the political and military organization that Aideed had built based upon that clan. The objective of the attack was to do as much damage to these people as possible, and they were given as little warning as the Pakistanis had been given earlier. No one is certain how many people were killed. This incident set the precedent, however, that this was not only a confrontation with the United Nations but with America.

Soon command-detonated mines began exploding under U.S. jeeps. The American response was to send in U.S. Army Rangers, which turned out to be a tremendous error. General Montgomery, the deputy U.N. commander and the commander of U.S. combat forces, would later testify before the Senate Armed Services Committee that U.S. forces were adequate to maintain security, but when the mission changed to target a particular faction, we did not have nearly enough military capability. The situation was not thought through any more than Lebanon was when the United States found itself in a similar situation. The Rangers, in trying to capture more and more of Aideed's people, ran into something no one had expected. People came from everywhere to fight the foreigners.

The first part of our intervention in Somalia, however, should not be overlooked, for it was a smashing success. It has largely been forgotten that one can in fact conduct a limited operation if it is planned correctly–if there is enough force and it is used only when absolutely necessary, if impartiality is clearly established, and if the country in question will solve its own problems with outside aid but not interference. This approach applies particularly to the case of Haiti.

The American response to the events of 3 October, when 18 U.S. Army Rangers were killed and the body of one was dragged through the streets of Mogadishu, was very similar to that following events in Lebanon 10 years earlier. In that case, our policy was reversed almost overnight and U.S. forces were pulled out. Likewise in Somalia, the U.S. policy was reversed. The President was, however, able to persuade Congress to give him six months before American troops had to be withdrawn, which was a considerable achievement.

It was at this point that I was called back, and the President expressed to me grave fear that if the United States pulled out of Somalia quickly, the situation would return to it's former state because all of the other forces would pull out as well. The future of U.N. peacekeeping would be destroyed, and it would touch off a wave of neo-isolationism in the United States. We talked about what could be done and decided that a gradual change would be best. U.S. forces could be built up in the short term to show that the United States would not be intimidated and also to try to improve the security situation. The other countries' forces would be encouraged to stay to provide stability. Furthermore, Aideed and his organization should be taken off the wanted list; they were a legitimate part of a Somali body politic whether the United States liked it or not. Unless the United States was going to occupy the country and change it by force, the Somalis had to sort out their own problems.

The U.S. domestic political reaction to Somalia was very strong, in part because no one had ever explained to the American people or to Congress exactly what was going on in Somalia. Americans were being killed, and no one could explain why they were fighting there or why they were a part of the United Nations' war. It is important to note that U.S. combat forces were at all times under U.S. command, never under U.N. command. At no time, until 3 October, did the U.S. policy objective for Somalia change from that of the United Nations. There were many reservations about it and a great deal of dialogue–the U.S. secretary of state argued with the U.N. secretary-general about whether to continue to pursue the U.N.'s approach. Because the argument was never resolved, however, the U.S. policy and the orders given to the U.S. forces on the ground never changed until 3 October, when the situation exploded.

The reaction of the administration, the Congress, and the public was that the United States should have nothing more to do with the mess the United Nations had made. When those 18 Rangers were killed, it was a shock effect. There had been six Americans killed during the first part of the operation, and a few others had died in accidents, but there had been no uproar or protests. People understood that they were there for a purpose–a reasonable purpose. The United States was taking all possible precautions to minimize casualties. People had expected many more, just as they had in the Gulf War. In this case, however, because few understood quite why U.S. forces were there, a sudden and large number of casualties occurring all at once produced an extremely strong reaction.

The effects of that reaction were first felt in U.S. policy toward Haiti. In October 1993, the United States, along with other countries such as Canada that were working on the Haiti problem, retreated to the old methods and decided to send a small, unarmed force into what was obviously a messy situation. When this force encountered resistance, the ship carrying them–the USS *Harlan County*, after which the incident was named–turned around and left. If a company of Marines had been sent with those 200 unarmed engineers, the forces would have landed and the United States would not have had to later send two aircraft carriers.

The fallout from Somalia caused the presidential document "Guidelines on Peacekeeping" to be rewritten. The administration backed away from its former, fairly aggressive approach. These developments were later reflected in the U.S. approach toward humanitarian intervention in Rwanda. Terrible things were happening in Rwanda. The United States looked at it and decided that it did not fit the President's new guidelines for peacekeeping. The situation was messy, and the United States did not see a good way to deal with it. It did not seem feasible that one could put together a force capable of stopping the conflict. The United States was therefore opposed to a peacekeeping force for Rwanda.

That position lasted about three weeks, and similar to the case of Somalia, the pressures began to build. So many people were being killed; someone needed to take action, and the United States was seen as blocking it. The United States finally agreed, slowly and grudgingly, to do something, and the idea eventually emerged to create a number of safe havens along the borders. There was so little enthusiasm for the idea, however, that it never really went anywhere. No one was putting up the money or the equipment. There was no U.S. president trying to recruit forces and, significantly, willing to pay for them, transport them, or provide equipment for them. The attitude was rather that the United States, while agreeing to be a part of the action, would not really play much of a role. Ultimately, nothing happened.

French television extensively covered the massacres and genocide in Rwanda, while American television only began coverage after the refugees began flowing into Zaire. The French had a guilty conscience because they had been supporting the previous Hutu regime, which was responsible for much of the violence. Therefore, the French felt that they had to respond earlier. They set up a safe haven in the southwestern part of the country, probably saving tens of thousands of people from being killed and preventing 100,000 more from fleeing into Zaire. Nonetheless, the earlier border plan was never put into effect; the issue lingered as the killings dragged on.

Finally, the combination of continued killings, CNN coverage of the carnage, and the tremendous flow of refugees into Zaire were enough to induce the United States to take action. The United States mounted a large military operation because no one else had the capability to deal with the situation. There were contingents from all over the world conducting humanitarian operations, but only the U.S. military could carry out such a massive operation in a hurry. The U.S. military would come to the aid of the various international and private organizations already there, such as the International Rescue Committee, CARE, World Vision, and others, as long as Americans were not put into a situation where they risked casualties. The United States had not wanted Americans directly involved in peacekeeping, but now the need to be more vigorous in helping put together a peacekeeping force for Rwanda was recognized. This delay, however, cost many Rwandan lives. It also produced a much larger flow of refugees into Zaire.

The ousted Hutu-led Rwandan regime, the army and the political leadership, then set up office in eastern Zaire. This regime is running the refugee camps; it is rebuilding its army and is preparing to go back in at some convenient stage, but it will not allow the refugees to return home because this move would take away the base in Zaire from which its return can be organized. Frankly, no one is willing to look at this problem. We are taking care of the refugees in the camps, but these refugees are really controlled by the previous Hutu regime. We are trying to build up the regime in Kigali and take care of the people remaining in Rwanda, but a time bomb is ticking on Zaire's side of the border. This is not a humanitarian issue. It is a political security issue that currently no one wants to recognize–not the United States, and certainly no one else. There is a potential for the repetition of mass tragedy, not only in Rwanda, but also next door in Burundi, yet another situation that no one wants to touch.

One of the lessons to be learned about humanitarian or political intervention in a country where anarchy reigns is that such intervention must occur quickly. If one moves early enough, skilled mediators and a modest force, in addition to the humanitarian element, may suffice. A peacekeeping force may not be needed. It is important that the first phase of an intervention contains a political, humanitarian, and security element, as was done in the first phase of the Somalia intervention. If an intelligent approach is taken, the security problems are minimized and the freedom of movement for the humanitarian element is maximized. If humanitarian activities are underway and the peacekeepers are not only protecting them but are also out there digging wells, running clinics, building roads, clearing irrigation ditches, and transporting food–as they were initially in Somalia–the peacekeepers will be seen by the general population as having a beneficial rather than a hostile purpose. Even those whose interests may be hurt will not be able to generate much opposition because their own people will see the help being offered.

Each element of the response thus reinforces the other, but they must be coordinated, and they must be thought through completely. To whom is assistance being provided? The humanitarians claim that aid has to reach everyone, even the people one does not like, unless one is prepared to take over and run the country, which is not advisable. The only place where the United States did that successfully was in Germany and Japan after the Second World War, which required a huge effort and expense of people, money, and political will.

Those who talk about reinstituting trusteeship or neo-colonialism are misguided because a country or organization should not just take over another country or even appear to do so, which is how the United Nations appeared to a number of Somalis. Aideed touched on a sympathetic chord by saying that the foreigners were telling the Somali people what to do. Most of the Somali people had serious reservations, and many of them were willing to fight either for Aideed or at least against the foreigners.

The same thing is true in other countries, so one must be extremely careful with massive military intervention for humanitarian purposes. Given the way both the world and this country are going, the United States will probably respond to crises that emerge sooner or later. Therefore, the United States ought to think about responding sooner, when it can reduce the magnitude of the problem if not actually solve it, thus reducing the degree of involvement required later. Nonetheless, it does not seem possible to establish a list of criteria that when in place determines the U.S. response. Such an evaluation is much more subjective, and it requires some sort of consensus between the Congress, the administration, the people, and even the media (particularly the television media).

Interestingly, responsiveness to the media over the past several years, whether the various administrations admit it or not, seems to have grown considerably. The media has had a great impact on policy. It seems to have made more policy decisions in the past three years than the policy planners, and this applies to Western Europe as well as the United States. That is part of the character of democracy, and one must take it into account. People have to come together and decide what they want to do or do not want to do, and in some cases this process will not be easy. The ability to reach consensus will evolve, but everyone needs to be more aware of the problems around the world and how the international community can best organize rapidly so as to minimize both the damage done and the costs to those trying to help.

From what I have seen in the fall of 1994, as the Clinton administration plans for action in Haiti, the lessons of Somalia are being taken extremely seriously. This includes plans to work energetically from day one to set up a neutral, reasonably disciplined police force. In Somalia, we knew that without a police force there would be no way to provide security for the people. The local Somali police were willing to go back out on the streets if they were protected from the warlords. A delegation of ten former police generals and colonels came to me and asked for help with transportation, training, and support in the event that they become involved in a situation beyond their ability to handle. Above all, they wanted support in keeping Aideed and Ali Mahdi under control. Both Washington and the United Nations, however, resisted the idea of building up a Somali police force, calling it nation-building. Those of us actually in Somalia disagreed, maintaining that it was absolutely indispensable. It was not nation-building because the Somalis were going to be in control, not us. Without it, someone would still have to provide security, and who would that be? It would be Americans patrolling in the back alleys. It would be much better to have Somalis in the back alleys. Ultimately, a police force was pulled together, but it was done locally with local resources. The United Nations was against this decision the entire time, so when the operation was transferred to the United Nations, the police force fell apart.

With the Haiti situation, the United States recognizes that Aristide's followers are not organized but still have the capacity for violence. They are facing a better organized regime under General Raoul Cedras, one with an army of sorts in addition to unofficial militias. If the United States plans to take away the weapons of the army and the militias, there had better be a police force to maintain order. The United States is working hard on this issue.

I am not saying that it is the right decision to go into Haiti, nor am I saying that the United States will be able to get the politics right, because it will be extremely tricky. I would say, however, that the most dangerous and most difficult part will be to resist getting sucked into remaking Haiti and to resist unconsciously choosing sides.

In Somalia, the conditions were created for the people to come together politically and modify or reaffirm agreements reached earlier. Instead, for the past six months they have spent their time jockeying for a stronger position before an interim government is created. Ambition and greed have surpassed common sense. In December 1993, there was a humanitarian conference in Addis Ababa, to which I brought Aideed. People did not particularly like him being there, but I maintained that there would never be peace in Somalia without Aideed's involvement in the peacemaking process. This raised some criticism from Washington. I responded that while Aideed was a bad guy, he was indispensable for peace, and I reminded them that not long ago they had Arafat on the south lawn of the White House. Arafat also was not particularly popular earlier, but he is indispensable to peace.

It may be that in the next couple of weeks Aideed will feel he has gotten strong enough to make a bid to take over the country. He cannot be another Siad Barre and run it all, however, so he will try to set up a series of alliances wherein he will be supported for the top job but will agree to leave his allies in charge elsewhere in the country. If that tactic is successful, the world will accept it rather than attempt to put in a U.S.-style democracy.

I suspect that deciding what the United States will settle for will be the dilemma in Haiti. Even when the United Nations takes over, everyone will still look to the United States to determine the outcome.

QUESTION: If I understand U.S. policy on Haiti correctly, it is to restore Aristide to power. In that sense, the United States seems to be taking political sides rather than coming in as a neutral force and letting the Haitians resolve their own political differences. Is this a built-in contradiction in U.S. policy?

MR. OAKLEY: It certainly is a contradiction, and I personally do not think that it is the way to solve Haiti's problems. Our objective to restore Aristide will, I suspect, produce many problems on the island. The United States will have to work hard to establish a position of support for Aristide up to a point, and they seem to be aware of the difficult job ahead of them. The potential dangers Aristide and his followers pose to those in opposition are not unlike the dangers they themselves face from those currently in authority. My hope is that a Haitian police force will be able to sort out this problem, and that they will not require Americans to do it for them. I do not think U.S. forces would be particularly effective at patrolling the back allies of Haiti. I doubt whether they could tell the good guys from the bad guys.

Apparently, Aristide hoped to be in charge of the police force now being created. When the United States refused his request, he asked that he at least be in charge of the selection process. This request was also refused. The selection and training of the police force and the establishment of their chain of command–with the development of loyalties inherent in this process–are all extremely important in maintaining their neutrality and their ability to ensure security on the island. The hope is that a police force will be created that reports to the United Nations–that is, to the United States–rather than to Aristide. Eventually, there would be real elections. For the time being, however, Aristide has been so equated with democracy that it will be difficult for the United States to maintain neutrality. If U.S. forces go in assuming that the actions of Aristide's followers are good and should automatically be supported, a tremendous backlash will occur.

NARRATOR: Where is the locus of thinking at any given time in the U.S. government's policy planning? Is it the National Security Council?

MR. OAKLEY: I am not a part of the Clinton administration, and I am as baffled as you are. On 6 October when I was called back on the Somalia issue by the Clinton administration, I sat down in the Cabinet room with President Clinton, Vice President Gore, and a dozen other people. We talked about how to get out of this terrible situation–the situation on Capitol Hill perhaps being worse than even that in Somalia. The next day we presented as plan to the congressional leadership. Until then there had been no serious thinking on the issue that I could detect. That lack of thinking is what had created this mess.

For a month, the administration's misgivings about the direction the intervention in Somalia was taking had been sufficiently strong enough for the secretary of state to argue with the U.N. secretary-general about it. Nonetheless, the course was not altered until the events of 3 October. The President claimed at that time to have made a prior decision to abandon the military course and pursue only a political course. If he had indeed made that prior decision, did he tell anyone? If he did make his decision known, why weren't the orders changed to the U.S. forces on the ground who were pursuing Aideed militarily?

The only solace I can offer is that the State Department seems to be pursuing its plans to remove Cedras and return Aristide to power in Haiti in a much more intelligent manner. Nongovernmental organizations containing people who actually know something about Latin America, Haiti, and humanitarian intervention are being consulted. The government has studied the lessons of Somalia. Two good analyses have been produced by the Defense Department, and the secretary of defense has seen them. The things that were carried out purely on an ad hoc basis in Somalia are now part of the actual planning process. Whether this means the operation will succeed, I do not know.

QUESTION: Do you think the members of Congress should vote on this invasion?

MR. OAKLEY: Interestingly, a total reversal of opinion between the parties now exists about whether Congress has to vote or not. Democrats now say a vote is not necessary, but they previously claimed to have been overridden on Grenada and Panama. Former President Bush did put the Gulf War to a vote.

There are differences of opinion as to what the War Powers Act means. The Republican administrations have strenuously defended the view that the president can send troops before reporting to Congress. The Democrats have tended to say that there must be congressional approval in advance. Now that the political roles are reversed, the positions are reversed.

It is conceivable that someone within the Clinton administration is Machiavellian enough to say that the Haiti invasion should be put to the vote in Congress, hoping that it will be voted down and then no action will have to be taken. This tactic would be an effective way of passing the buck.

NARRATOR: Secretary Eagleburger said you would give a memorable analysis of the main elements in this situation, and you have. We hope that as the years go by, there will be more Bob Oakleys in the foreign service. Thank you for an excellent presentation.

CHAPTER SIX

Somalia: Reflections on U.S. Intervention*

STEVENSON McILVAINE

NARRATOR: Stevenson McIlvaine began his involvement in Somalia in the fall of 1992 as the notetaker in policy meetings hosted by the Department of State's Africa Bureau. He chronicled the growing frustration of policymakers in the State Department as people continued to die of hunger in Somalia despite a U.S. military airlift of food to the region. He ran the night shift of the Somalia task force for the first two weeks of the U.S.-led United Task Force and in June 1993 was named deputy chief of mission of the U.S. Liaison Office in Mogadishu.

When he left Somalia in July 1994, Mr. McIlvaine had served four ambassadors in a very trying period, often full of risks and hazards to the participants involved. He negotiated with warlords and mass murderers and prepared the ground for Ambassador Robert Oakley's efforts to secure the release of an American airman. He also conducted three weeks of successful maneuvers to gain the release of an American journalist held hostage by Somali gunmen. He lived in a trailer in a military camp surrounded by 50 U.S. Marines, yet managed to travel through much of the country and most of Mogadishu. He returned to the Africa Bureau in September 1994 and became responsible for the planning of the evacuation of U.N. forces still in Somalia. He expects to be

**Presented in a Forum at the Miller Center of Public Affairs on 15 March 1995.*

appointed to a deputy chief position in Lusaka, Zambia, sometime in the summer of 1995.

As a Foreign Service officer, Mr. McIlvaine has served in Vietnam, Egypt, Guinea-Bissau, Zaire, and Tanzania. He is a graduate of Harvard College and served in the U.S. Army, worked for a member of Congress, wrote for Virginia weekly newspapers, and was active in Virginia politics. He won election to and served one term on the Fauquier County Board of Supervisors. As someone who has gone to the school of the statesman and the diplomat, Mr. McIlvaine has much to tell us about Somalia, diplomacy, and politics in general.

MR. McILVAINE: My Somali history began two years ago with the Regional Affairs Office of the Africa Bureau, where I was the bureau labor adviser, better known as the utility infielder–one who picks up all of the loose balls and all of the loose jobs. The loose job at the time dealt with the mess in Somalia. I began as the notetaker for the policy meetings at the time of the airlift in September 1992. That effort led to the operation center and the mounting frustration that precipitated President Bush's decision at Thanksgiving to send American troops into Somalia. Despite the airlift and other efforts, the food was still not getting to the starving people. Thugs, gangs, bandits, factions, militiamen, and others were stealing the food and selling it. UNITAF, the American-led U.N. operation, for the first four months of 1993 broke the back of that militia operation, delivered food to the starving people, and stopped the famine, although it very carefully and by design did not deal with the underlying problems with the militia and the establishment of normal political processes. That job was left to UNOSOM, the United Nations operation that took over in May 1993. I arrived a month and a half later, after UNOSOM had already entered a major shooting war with General Mohamed Farah Aideed, the most prominent of the warlords. Events then rapidly turned sour, culminating on the first Sunday night in October. That night I was sitting on the roof of our bunkerlike "imitation embassy" with the communicator, watching what was obviously an horrific fire fight several miles away. This was the 3 October battle of the Olympic Hotel during which some 18 Americans were killed. At that point

I was running the embassy as chargé because the ambassador had been called back to Washington for consultation. Within days it was clear that the ambassador was not returning. Robert Oakley arrived to negotiate a truce. At the time, an American airman was being held hostage by the Somalis after his helicopter was shot down. A Nigerian soldier was being held hostage as well. Overall, policy was nearing collapse.

We gradually put it all back together in a mad scramble. We negotiated the release of both hostages and began a process of political negotiations with Mohamed Farah Aideed and the other warlords. Six weeks later, Ambassador Bogosian, the new resident ambassador, arrived. He stayed until the end of May 1994, and a month later Ambassador Simpson took over and still works in Nairobi as director of the Somalia Liaison Office. The embassy was moved out of Mogadishu in September, and I left at the end of July. Since my return, I have worked with Ambassador Simpson on the process of getting the United Nations safely out of Somalia, once we had decided that a year's worth of hard work to reach a political conclusion with the warlords had failed.

In the summer of 1993 the United States unsuccessfully tried force, and for the remainder of 1993 and almost all of 1994, it tried and failed at negotiations. Finally, 1995 was spent getting everyone out. I am pleased to say that two weeks ago we finished the job without casualties. Two people remain in Nairobi to keep an eye on Somalia, and a small aid mission remains to keep track of events and to help avoid another famine.

Somalia exhibits a fragile stability with a medieval flavor. Having broken down and been destroyed in four years of civil war, government no longer exists in Somalia. In its place one finds regional and local arrangements through elders, local chieftains, or warlords. These leaders have brought a certain amount of stability and order to various regions of the country. The capital city of Mogadishu remains turbulent. The capital is still bitterly contested because it has the only two consistent sources of revenue–the airport and the seaport–and whoever or whatever goes in and out can be taxed. Mogadishu is still the symbol of government. A tenuous peace has continued in Mogadishu since the completion of the withdrawal on 3 March, and the two factions are working together. No one is willing to claim a victory yet or say that they have made peace, but the situation is more promising than the press and many other observers expected. It is now completely up to the Somalis to do what they see fit.

QUESTION: Who today could perhaps say, "I told you so"?

MR. McILVAINE: Smith Hempstone, the former editor of the *Washington Times* and the ambassador to Kenya appointed by the Bush administration, wrote an annoyingly prescient cable in 1992 called "The Somalia Tarbaby," which was leaked to the press. Sadly, he was on target with lines like "If you like Beirut, you'll love Somalia." He argued that the intervention would not work and that the Somalis would never agree to anything no matter what we did to them. That argument proved to be close to the truth.

QUESTION: Is there a lesson from the Somalia situation that can be used as a model or an example for the future?

MR. McILVAINE: There are many lessons, the most obvious one being that the United Nations is not ready for this kind of operation. The background of U.N. involvement goes back to the Congo emergency in the early 1960s. Since then, the United Nations experienced the postcolonial era of all of the new countries that came into the United Nations and the growth of the nonaligned movement. The United States was suddenly outvoted in the United Nations, and the United States and Western European powers could no longer effectively use the United Nations for their purposes as they had previously, to the point where Khrushchev pounded his shoe on the table in frustration. The United Nations became a rather ineffectual Third World employment society. Then the Cold War ended and issues like the situations in Somalia and Bosnia arose. The United States depended on the United Nations to handle these situations, but the United Nations did not know how.

U.N. action can work the way it was done in Iraq and during the first phase in Somalia. In both cases, one country (the United States) was the dominant player, taking the lead under a vague U.N. imprimatur. The French have taken the lead occasionally in corners of Africa. When one Western power takes the lead and is willing to run the operation, it can be done effectively. The United Nations alone can monitor the situation and can be a presence, but it cannot make things happen or make peace. That is the pragmatic side.

The policy side of the question is whether or not it is possible to make peace and whether other countries should even try. The answer from Somalia is "probably not." No matter what the United States did, it wasn't able to make peace until the people of Somalia were ready to do it themselves. The same lesson applied in Lebanon. In Lebanon, once everyone left after ten years of intense international involvement, the Lebanese made some sort of settlement themselves. In Afghanistan, however, the outside troops left but everyone is still fighting, so I'm not sure what the model is.

NARRATOR: What about the British in east Africa? Have conditions changed so drastically that what the British did almost a century ago is now no longer conceivable?

MR. McILVAINE: Neo-colonialism is the specter you raise. Neo-colonialism is considered a dirty word, but many people would be delighted to have any kind of order reestablished, colonial or otherwise, in this world of "failed states." I cannot see the United States or any other country taking that approach. The French are tempted by such involvement, but they would only do it where intervention was fairly small, cheap, and manageable. Any such involvement is a variation on action by a dominant power under a U.N. imprimatur but not run by the United Nations.

QUESTION: Will an attempt be made to feed the Somali children, or do you think the starvation will return?

MR. McILVAINE: The starvation will not return for a while. That problem was addressed successfully. The people had a good harvest and they now have reasonable order in most of the country. Unlike in 1992, the farmers can farm and harvest their crops as a result of the combined U.S.-U.N. effort. If that order does not hold, however, and if the gunmen in Mogadishu start marauding again through the countryside, it is possible to return to the starting point. What has been accomplished is fragile, and I think everyone–the Somali people in particular–recognizes that fact.

QUESTION: Would events have taken a different turn if the United Nations had had an effective military staff reporting to the Security Council?

MR. McILVAINE: The problem is not so much the individuals as it is the command structure. General Montgomery, the American deputy commander of UNOSOM, had never had an experience like this one. He is a career American Army officer, now a three-star general, and he is used to issuing orders and seeing results. That did not happen with the United Nations in Somalia. An order was issued and it was negotiated with each contingent, who then went back to their home capital. The United States was the worst of all because it made a major fetish of not taking orders from any other nationality. The United States would not do it, and neither would the French or Italians. Soon no one would, and every order had to be negotiated. No one was willing to cede total command authority over their troops to an international bureaucracy.

QUESTION: As I understand the situation, there is no military staff advising the Security Council on how to make plans, issue orders, or organize forces. If such a staff were in existence, would the outcome have been different?

MR. McILVAINE: It is true that each country is responsible for handling its own involvement. The United Nations is finally beginning to develop a structure to deal with this problem. A U.N. military staff would have made the setting up easier, but the operation would not have been any different because the contingents remain unwilling to take orders from foreigners.

QUESTION: Isn't the specter of starvation enough to motivate a dominant power to move in under the mantle of the United Nations as the United States did in the Gulf War?

MR. McILVAINE: It is and it isn't. I am now working on Rwanda, and tomorrow I have to go to New York with another ambassador and talk to the United Nations about what should be done in that country. Rwanda is a case where the genocide was portrayed on television all over the world just as starvation in Somalia was. It caught everyone's attention, but no one moved in to help in large part because of the Somalia experience. The massacres ran their course.

The U.S. government and most of the Western powers are caught between two horns of this dilemma. First, people in the United States want to help others; they do not want to see millions starve or millions die in man-made disasters around the world. They want to help, particularly if it is shown on television. If it is not on television, people cannot notice such problems. Angola has been murderous for 20 years, and the international response has been muted because Angola has never made it on television.

Second, the United States certainly does not want to use the big stick of the American military. People here do not want to send in U.S. troops, and they certainly do not want any U.S. casualties. As a result, in all of these crises produced by thugs of one stripe or another–be they Serbian thugs, Somali thugs, or Hutu or Tutsi thugs in Rwanda–the United States has no way of disciplining them, knocking them back, shutting them up, or putting them out of action because this country will not use force. People worry about starvation and murder, but their response to these crises is to exhort. This is a major issue for the Defense Department and the U.S. government. They struggle over whether there is a way to use military power effectively in such cases or whether the United States should just accept the fact that military power is not useful and not a good idea in these situations.

QUESTION: Isn't that really a decision for the American people to make? It is not a question for the United Nations, the administration, or the Defense Department. A consensus must be obtained from the people demonstrating their willingness to go the limit.

MR. McILVAINE: I basically agree, but how does one begin such a debate? Should it be done through leadership, with political leaders making the decisions on what should be done, or should the U.S. government wait for the people to say, "You must do it." In the case of the starvation in Somalia and the genocide in Rwanda, my impression was that there was an outburst of popular feeling that something should be done. Whether one would call that a popular mandate or not, I leave it for each of you to decide.

On the other hand, once something did happen in Somalia and Americans were killed, there was an outburst, at least in Congress, to get American troops out, which is what happened. A leadership question is involved in deciding what is in the best interest of the United States and then seeing if popular support can be built for the necessary policy.

NARRATOR: Why do you think that did not happen in quite that way with the Belgian Congo? Was that a leadership issue, or was it early in the United Nations when people were more tolerant and the United States had a majority on the Security Council?

MR. McILVAINE: The United States had better control of the United Nations because it had a Security Council bloc and the Russians had not yet started using their veto. They did not use it on the Congo, at any rate. In addition, the Congo was caught up in the Cold War dynamic. The United States could not let this huge country in the center of a newly arising independent area go communist. Thirty years later, that situation seems a bit laughable because what did "going communist" mean in central Africa? Nonetheless, that was a major concern at the time. That operation did work reasonably well. The United States established a kind of order that held that incredibly inchoate country together for years.

QUESTION: Reflecting on popular opinion, my recollection at the time the United States went into Somalia initially as a U.N.-led force, and even at the time it turned the problem over to the United Nations, is that there was substantial public support. People were hopeful and had been impressed by the success of stopping the starvation. Even when the United Nations began its operations, people seemingly were in favor of it as a general proposition. Haiti is an interesting counterexample. This administration moved into Haiti in September 1994 while, by and large, the polls showed a substantial opposition to involvement. In Somalia, was there ever any prospect of it succeeding? You indicated that the United Nations was not really equipped to do the kind of nation-building that it undertook. Had the United States continued a U.S.-led operation in nation-building after stopping the starvation, was there any prospect of success?

MR. McILVAINE: In hindsight, I think it was not going to work. I would have argued, however, that it had to be given a chance. By the end of last year, I had personally given it a year's worth of hard work and had seen each effort get to the edge and then fall apart. This happened largely because General Aideed would not accept a deal with any rivals but yet was not quite strong enough to take care of the situation himself. There was popular support for America's efforts. Americans wanted to "do good," which is a basic instinct around the world. Once it came down to costing U.S. lives, however, the public was not willing to go that far. That sentiment became vividly clear once the shooting war with Aideed began. He learned quickly that he won if the U.S. troops killed Somalis and he won if he killed Americans; the United States lost in either case. It took a while for the United States to realize that it could not win.

QUESTION: There is a military expression known as "instant and devastating retaliation." Was the command on the ground able to make that decision quickly, or did a relay have to be sent to the State Department or the Pentagon to get the clearance?

MR. McILVAINE: Speaking personally as a nonmilitary person, one of the military mistakes made was forgetting the lesson of Desert Storm–you give the field commander everything he needs and then get out of his way. The commander is allowed to make the decisions, and he either succeeds or fails and is hung if he fails or receives medals if he succeeds. That lesson was forgotten in the Somalia situation.

QUESTION: What has the United States learned from these experiences that can be applied in the future, with the United States either acting on its own or through the United Nations. What approach should be taken in the future?

MR. McILVAINE: Some important issues are emerging, such as assessing macromanagement on a tactical level or on a grand-strategy level and if there needs to be one-nation-led interventions with U.N. sanction. The question of political support also arises. For this country to do something effectively, particularly to risk troops, it has to have political support. There are many more issues than that with which the United States is grappling. In the Africa Bureau there never seems to be enough time to think about any of these things because we always seem to have a new crisis on our hands. Two days after the ships left Somalia, I was trying to learn about Rwanda and make headway on that situation. One major question involves determining what the U.S. interest is and how much the United States is willing to commit to these messy, post-Cold War problems. Some people say the United States has no interest elsewhere and it should avoid intervention. Some say the United States must do something in Bosnia or Rwanda. There is no clear consensus. As taxpayers, I think people need to think about what they want the government to do.

QUESTION: What is the prognosis if the United States does nothing?

MR. McILVAINE: The alternative to using military force when dealing with thugs is to say, "This is not in our interest; it is not important to us; it is awful, but we are just going to turn our backs and let it happen." Politically, the United States does not seem to be able to say that. In the case of Haiti, the United States does have an interest there. Haiti is very close to the United States, and the United States gets the spillover. A functioning, stable, and developing Haiti is very much in the U.S. interest. A functioning, stable, and developing Somalia is almost irrelevant to the United States except that this country still pays a major share of the cost of such a breakdown. The United States generally pays 25 percent of the cost of the U.N. system for disaster relief and refugees.

COMMENT: You raised an interesting question with your word *leadership*. It reminds me of an op-ed piece that Brent Scowcroft and Arnold Kanter wrote in the *Washington Post* in early 1995 about six weeks ago. They argued that the United States must show more leadership in the world. Leadership in that context really means that a country must be willing to use military force and economic power. The United States does not have as much economic power as it used to have, and economic power does not seem to be as effective as it once was. In terms of military power, the United States only has it when there is a national consensus that it is going to win, such as in the Persian Gulf War. If one believes, as I do, that major force should not be used unless the issue if vital, then as one looks at the world today, particularly in Africa, not much is vital to the United States. If this premise is accepted, then the question of "using leadership" becomes irrelevant, if leadership means in that context the use of force or economic power.

MR. McILVAINE: An interesting op-ed piece by Jessica Matthews also appeared recently in the *Washington Post*. She raised the issue of the romantic attachment to the 1950s when the United States was unquestionably the big guy on the block and all our government had to do was say things and people jumped. That is no longer the case. The United States does not have the overpowering economic power it exercised in the 1950s and is unwilling to use military power, quite rightly, unless there is a vital interest at stake.

One way to handle problems that arise, although it is politically unfashionable right now, is through those multilateral organizations in which the United States is a major player and funder–the IMF, the World Bank, and the United Nations and its agencies. World problems that eventually will either cost the United States money or have an impact on it can be handled if these organizations can be made to work reasonably effectively and if a consensus can be obtained among the European powers, China, and some other representatives of the Third World. Achieving consensus on what is good for the world in global environment, population, and refugee issues—all issues that eventually hurt us but where the direct national interest is not obvious—is an important part of leadership.

NARRATOR: Are those areas where the model of the single-nation-led task force is not enough?

MR. McILVAINE: These are issues that do not require an intervention but require a long-term management.

COMMENT: In the post-World War II world, the United States was willing to call people like the Cuban dictator Batista allies. The American people had a singular vital interest, which was to contain communism in the Cold War, so they were willing to support and fund regimes that behaved much like communist governments. Today, people who act in a similar way in their own countries with their own people are now referred to as Stalinist.

MR. McILVAINE: Diplomats need to be very careful about becoming too self-righteous or sounding too principled, because they often deal in expediency. If one has to deal with a thug to get a job done, so be it. In my minor role, when an Associated Press correspondent was being held hostage in Mogadishu, I dealt with a variety of petty thugs, including a man nicknamed "Colonel Shortneck," to try to put pressure on the people holding her so she would be released. These are not people that would have been invited to anyone's drawing room. Eventually, I found the right combination of buttons to push and thugs to build alliances with to get her released.

From a historical perspective, one should be careful how one uses the word *thug*. Was the great warrior king, Prince Edward, a thug? He probably was. He was certainly murderous and bloodthirsty, and I am sure the French did not see him in any favorable light. Thugs can become great national leaders when they win, and the definition can change.

QUESTION: Would you disagree with the statement that it is highly unlikely in the foreseeable future that the United States will be the leading nation in any major military intervention unless truly vital national interests are at stake? Any smart leader these days is aware of the fact that support can disappear in a wink and be manipulated by either CNN or some demagogue.

MR. McILVAINE: CNN is a tremendous influence on policy these days. I do not know the answer to your question. Certainly I was not smart enough to say in 1988 that in two years the United States would have a U.S. Army charging through the sands of Iraq. I hesitate to predict the future, but I think your point is valid that any American leader will need to be careful about commitment of U.S. forces. In part, that is the lesson of Somalia. Somalia has put that stamp on the use of U.S. forces. I think it is not necessarily the right stamp but is a fact of political life.

NARRATOR: The cyclical theory may be something to keep in mind in terms of how categorical the United States is about the role it will play. After World War I, the United States won the war and then withdrew, claiming Europe was none of its business. After World War II, however, there has always been a cyclical character to U.S. involvement.

COMMENT: I think the national interest can come into question on the North Korean situation to some degree. The United States has many military people ready to act in a situation where the national interest could be questioned.

MR. McILVAINE: What drives policy in North Korea is the nuclear proliferation question.

COMMENT: But even the nuclear question is a very regional concern at this point in time. North Korea has no capability to strike beyond Japan or China.

MR. McILVAINE: It is one of those unimaginable frontiers. If someone actually drops a nuclear bomb on someone else, what will happen? Is that it, or does the incident trigger a series of events stretching around the world?

QUESTION: I see a distinct difference between the Gulf War and the Somalia situation. The Gulf War was an outright aggression, and the United Nations was obligated to do something about it. The U.N. Charter guarantees national borders, as I understand the Charter, so an obligation existed, and the United States just happened to have a plan handy.

Concerning the earlier point made about a military staff, had there been a staff in existence, an alert staff would have had a contingency plan prepared. The United States government has many such plans for different areas of the world. The commander arrangements would all be set, with a clear line from the Security Council through the military staff down to the senior military person in the country. The confusion in Somalia would have been eliminated because military commanders would have had a straight, single line of communication to the people that issue the orders. Wouldn't that make a difference?

MR. McILVAINE: Some of what you have said is absolutely true and would have helped. The United Nations is improving and is developing some military expertise from the Somalia situation. You are not addressing the basic problem, however, which is placing the forces under the command of anyone else without a veto.

NARRATOR: One word that has not been mentioned is communism. Is there any possibility that the kind of role communism played as a mobilizing force could ever be played by Islam in Turkey, Algeria, and other places? Some people say that it does not have the same characteristics, but the news from Turkey suggests that it is a dynamic force. Does Islam play a role in Africa?

MR. McILVAINE: If people declare Islam an enemy the way they declared communism an enemy, that would be declaring war on the entire Islamic world. I do not think they want to do that. In many ways, Islamic fundamentalists do good things. The problem is that they tend to view Americans as the Great Satan and the source of all evil and to produce regimes that are hostile to us, such as Sudan or Iran. The United States is grappling with that problem, and it must somehow avoid making all of Islam an enemy.

QUESTION: One issue that must be faced is the basic question of whether failing or failed states can become a growing problem to the United States. In other words, if they are not a vital interest now, will they become one?

MR. McILVAINE: We touched on that question in terms of looking for other areas where this problem might occur. As an Africanist, I recognize plenty of candidates. The one candidate for failure that everyone mentions is Zaire. I served twice in Zaire and have always been fascinated by that country. Zaire is one of the largest countries in Africa. It is the Bantu heartland; it is the Congo River basin; it is the source of 50 percent of African art. Zaire is a tremendously alive, vital place, but it is almost ungovernable. There is no infrastructure, railroads, or roads. There is no way to get from one end of the country to the other except in the most primitive ways that Stanley used 100 years ago. Despite these problems, however, Zaire seems to be surviving, but don't tell anyone! A little historical perspective is useful. It is good to remember that throughout Africa, the colonial era started just 90 years ago, so many African nations have only had 30 years of independence under their own attempts at modern Western-style government. Many countries are influenced by loosely rooted inheritance from a colonial power, often the British or French parliamentary system. The influence is not deeply felt, however.

The best scenario for Somalia is that the local traditional leadership will gradually assume command, and Somalia will return to the Middle Ages, in a metaphorical sense. It will go back to societies where there is little connection with the outside and local rule predominates. Maybe they can gradually build up their own indigenous forms of government that are meaningful and useful for them.

NARRATOR: We are grateful to you for taking us inside the Somali problem. It is immensely helpful to have someone share their experience with us who has actually been there and faced it with courage.

CHAPTER SEVEN

Limitations to United Nations Peacemaking in Africa*

THOMAS P. SHEEHY

NARRATOR: Thomas Sheehy was a highly regarded graduate student at the University of Virginia and was an editor at the Miller Center. After receiving his master's degree in international relations from the University of Virginia, he joined the staff of the Heritage Foundation, where he is presently the Jay Kingham Fellow in International Regulatory Affairs. He has been the author of several of the Heritage Foundation's publications as well as other magazine articles and op-ed pieces. Tom writes on international economic development and trade issues, U.N. peacekeeping, and Africa. He has also appeared on television and spoken on radio programs, including ABC News and National Public Radio, and has testified before committees of Congress on proposals to reform U.S. foreign aid.

Tom has had the unique experience of being an election observer in Kenya and an election assessment officer in Tanzania, working with the International Republican Institute. He has traveled widely in Africa, recently returning from a trip to observe U.N. peacekeeping in Western Sahara. He has also worked a summer at the Kumasi Brewery Ltd. while residing at the Kumasi University in Ghana. In addition to his discussion on Rwanda, he will also be making some general comments about U.N. peace-keeping in Africa.

**Presented in a Forum at the Miller Center of Public Affairs on 19 August 1994.*

MR. SHEEHY: In my discussion today, I will address the Rwanda conflict within the overall context of U.N. peacekeeping. I will briefly describe the strife and conflict occurring throughout Africa, the international community's role in Africa, and the prospects for resolution of these tragic conflicts.

Much of the conventional wisdom concerning Africa is that tribal conflict or civil war can be attributed to the end of the Cold War. Both the United States and the Soviet Union had supported their respective clients throughout the continent for strategic reasons. For better or worse, the superpower "patrons" kept a lid on things.

That analysis is generally valid. For example, I doubt that Somalia would have been allowed to erupt into tribal or clan conflict if the Soviets and the Americans were still vying for strategic superiority in the Horn of Africa. On the other hand, the end of the Cold War has also brought some opportunities for peace throughout Africa. Mozambique, for example, was involved in a civil war for 15 years, and now there is movement toward elections and hope for peace. The whole dynamic in southern Africa is generally favorable for a democratic transformation, at least so far. I am highly doubtful that this change could have occurred if the Soviet Union were still competing with the United States for influence in that region. With the elimination of the Soviet factor in southern Africa, the regime in Pretoria had greater freedom to move ahead with a democratic transition. I do not believe that would have happened if the African National Congress (ANC) were still seen as a vehicle for Soviet expansionism.

Unfortunately, several of the Cold War conflicts, or what is perceived as Cold War conflicts, are still raging. The conflict in Angola, which was seen primarily as a proxy war between the United States and the Soviet Union for many years, fits into this category. The United States no longer supports Jonas Savimbi, and the Russians no longer support the Marxist government in Angola, yet Angola is still war-torn and literally hundreds of thousands of people are dying there. My point is that the roots of conflict in Africa are manifold, going beyond the role of the superpowers. The tribal aspect is very real and is often given a great deal of attention. Even traditionally stable states such as Kenya are suffering terrible tribal conflict and a high degree of civil unrest. In Rwanda, the tribal element certainly plays a role in the struggle over limited resources between the Tutsis and the Hutus.

Another important point to remember in analyzing conflict in Africa, tribal or otherwise, is the key role the state has played since independence. Economic power has been concentrated within the government both for practical reasons, such as the departure of expatriate communities following independence and the need to consolidate central authority, and for strong ideological reasons, such as the commitment to socialism. For many years this socialist-statist orientation was supported by foreign aid donors in the West, people who presumably held pro-capitalist sentiments. As a result, the goal for anyone in Africa was to control the state because that was where the money was. In most African countries, success in private business was not seen as a viable alternative. A great deal of conflict has naturally resulted as various factions compete for control of the government. This factor in African politics and development has not been given enough analysis or emphasis. Fortunately, the statist approach is losing favor. A general move toward free markets and liberalization has occurred with the support of the IMF and the World Bank. This is a positive development, and some good economic results are visible in a few countries, such as Ghana and Uganda.

As the superpowers have disengaged from Africa, the United Nations has become more engaged. There has been a proliferation of so-called peacekeeping operations. Six operations are currently underway in Africa by my count, with plans for additional ones in Zaire and Sudan. Peacekeeping has become a major growth industry, and the United Nations has been overwhelmed. Unlike peacekeeping of the traditional sort where lightly armed peacekeepers are introduced only after the various parties have agreed to make peace, a much more assertive notion of peacekeeping has been put forth in recent years. Conflicts are no longer seen as the responsibility of the superpowers, but rather are now deemed to be within the United Nations' "sphere of influence." U.N. Secretary General Boutros Boutros-Ghali has put forth an aggressive notion of peacemaking, not just peacekeeping. No longer would U.N.

forces necessarily have the cooperation of the belligerents; they would sometimes be interjected into civil conflicts.

This was essentially what happened in Somalia. Historically, the United Nations has had a rather poor record of peacekeeping or peacemaking in Africa. For example, the U.N. intervention in the Congo in the early 1960s turned into a disaster after it became a proxy war between the superpowers. Somalia became a test case for the post-Cold War era. President Bush made the initial commitment of troops, and President Clinton broadened the commitment to include nation-building–a long-term commitment to rebuilding society in Somalia. Unfortunately, the U.N. operation in Somalia has pretty much collapsed and is being withdrawn. What little hope there is for future stability in Somalia rests on more traditional means, such as elders and tribal leaders coming together and working out a stable peace.

The United Nations was not particularly successful in Angola either. U.N. personnel were responsible for overseeing the election between UNITA (National Union for the Total Independence of Angola) and the MPLA (Popular Movement for the Liberation of Angola). Unfortunately, there were not many U.N. troops on the ground in Angola, and UNITA returned to the battlefield after it lost the election. The country is suffering a terrible civil war once again.

The situation in Western Sahara is illustrative of the United Nations' many problems. Western Sahara was a Spanish colony until Spain withdrew in 1975. Morocco quickly annexed the territory, but that annexation was never officially recognized by the international community. There was a displacement of certain indigenous peoples and a sporadic war of resistance with Morocco for control of the territory. In 1989 the Moroccans and the rebel organization Polisario, largely composed of indigenous Western Saharans who fled to Algeria, signed an agreement to hold a U.N.-supervised referendum on the future of Western Sahara. The question was, would Western Sahara be integrated into Morocco or would it become an independent country run by the Polisario? In the course of its peacemaking efforts, the United Nations has been manipulated by Morocco. Essentially, King Hassan of Morocco agreed to have a referendum to get the Polisario to stop fighting, but then he deliberately let the referendum process drag out. The referendum was supposed to be held in 1991, but it has not yet taken place. The United Nations has brought a modicum of peace to Western Sahara, but it is not fostering the reconciliation that will be necessary for a long-term solution between Morocco and the Polisario. The Polisario has become very disillusioned by the United Nations because it sees it as having been manipulated by Morocco.

The U.S. approach to the United Nations over the last several years has been naive. Whether it be in Angola, Somalia, or Western Sahara, there was a notion that the United Nations could be a neutral force for good and thus bring to an end many civil conflicts. This did not happen in Somalia because the United Nations was always perceived as either serving the interests of General Aideed, Ali Mahdi, or the Italians. The United Nations was unable to limit itself to delivering relief supplies and being a neutral referee in this civil conflict. Similarly, in Western Sahara as well as in Angola, the United Nations has never been perceived as being neutral. The Polisario has viewed it as an agent of Morocco and France, and UNITA always felt that because the MPLA-run government controlled the oil, the United Nations was biased in the government's favor. It is important to remember that the United Nations always represents someone's interest in the minds of the various belligerents. This is the problem with all peacemaking operations.

Although I am critical of the performance of the United Nations in recent years, it has been placed unfairly in many of these difficult situations. Nevertheless, they have many of their own bureaucratic problems. The organization is terribly inefficient. The United Nations has 90,000 peacekeeping troops deployed throughout the world, several times greater than the previous year. Logistically, fulfilling this vastly expanded responsibility has become a great challenge.

The U.N. experience in Rwanda illustrates my point. France had been the traditional outside power in much of Africa and has had long-standing interests in that part of the world. France has always been far more involved in Africa than the United States, which never had any major interests in Africa.

Last year French forces were in Rwanda tacitly supporting the Hutu government in the civil war against the Tutsi-dominated Rwanda Patriotic Front (RPF). The United States and other countries wanted a multinational U.N. peacekeeping force to go in and bring a closure to the civil war, and so the French were essentially pressured out of Rwanda. In spring 1994 when the mass killings began in Rwanda, the United Nations could not muster an intervention force because various countries did not want to send their troops there, so the French army returned. They have successfully created a "no-go zone," which has been effective in enabling workers to carry out their life-saving humanitarian mission.

I remember having a discussion with a member of the RPF, which is now running the government in Rwanda, just after the United Nations announced it would send in troops. I asked this person his opinion of the French, who I thought were playing a rather constructive role in the country. The RPF, however, wanted France to withdraw as soon as possible. France had a historical role in that country, and it was not perceived as being sympathetic to the RPF government. I pointed out to the RPF representative that Rwanda would probably not get a U.N. force to do the same type of humanitarian work as the French were doing. I said to him very bluntly, "Your problem is not with the French. The Rwandan problem is among Rwandans, and for the RPF to claim that somehow France cannot play a constructive role in their country because they've traditionally been allied with the government I think is a real problem. If you are telling me that Hutus and Tutsis cannot come together in Rwanda, then it really does not matter whether the French are there or whether it's a multinational force of Ghanaian and Zimbabwean troops."

For peace to prevail, the belligerents must be willing to give peace a chance. If the French can play a constructive role, so be it. They should be encouraged to do so. The Clinton administration is slowly coming around to that position, but unfortunately, the French are making plans to depart. I am not very optimistic that the U.N. force planned for Rwanda will play a constructive role in that country.

I believe that in the next five to ten years, people will realize that the United Nations has vastly overplayed its hand in terms of peacemaking operations. There will be a tendency for powers to act unilaterally. The last several years have been somewhat of an aberration with respect to the Clinton administration's strong ideological commitment to multilateralism. Most high-ranking administration officials come from academia and have had some grandiose ideas about the role of the United Nations. We are now seeing the bankruptcy of some of those ideas. Unilateral action such as the French humanitarian relief in Rwanda will become the usual mode of intervention. The French operation in Rwanda should be applauded. The notion that the French cannot act nobly in Africa because they have national interests there must be set aside.

I am trying to tie this point together with the erroneous notion that the United Nations represents no country's national interests. Such a disinterested cosmopolitan entity does not exist and never has. The United Nations cannot be such an entity. French motives in Rwanda may not be entirely pure, but what they have accomplished there is generally positive.

Charles Krauthammer recently wrote a provocative column entitled "The Death of the Monroe Doctrine" in which he criticizes the Clinton administration's position toward Haiti. On one hand the administration is making the case that Haiti is a vital U.S. national interest, yet it still rules out invading Haiti unless it is done within the context of a clear United Nations mandate. There is a fundamental contradiction here. Krauthammer argues that when national interests are at stake and the cause is just, nations should feel free to act and defend those interests. The whole U.N. framework that has been developed assiduously by the Clinton administration, Boutros-Ghali, and others over the last several years, distorts the proper functioning of interests. This multilateral approach is counterproductive. The French were asked to leave Rwanda under the faulty assumption that the United Nations could do a better job because it would not be serving national interests.

Although I paint a rather pessimistic picture of the future of Africa, there are some positive developments. If South Africa can make the transition to democracy, it could play a positive role in the southern African region similar to the role the French have played in Rwanda. South Africa has a modern military and a direct economic and political interest in southern Africa. It already has become more involved in trying to mediate the Angolan civil war. If President Mandela can get the country's affairs in order, South Africa might be able to play a positive peacekeeping role in Africa. On the other hand, Nigeria's intervention in Liberia through the U.N.-sponsored regional force has not been particularly successful.

There has also been a willingness recently to talk about fundamental issues that have been taboo for many years in Africa. For example, although the Organization of African Unity (OAU) Charter expressly forbids the redrawing of national boundaries, it is now at least possible to talk about it. Independence has been achieved by Eritrea, which seceded from Ethiopia after a lengthy civil war. That action was unprecedented and raises the question of how to handle such changes in the future. In closing, my fundamental point is that the international community can play a positive role in resolving conflicts, but people must be realistic about its inherent limitations.

QUESTION: Your comments seem to presume an indefinite continuation of general instability and that the United Nations or one of the major powers would simply have to intervene. What are the prospects for the development of stable indigenous regimes—something that looks like a democratic order? You spoke of the tendency toward statism. What are the key characteristics of these states? Is there any prospect of what can be regarded as normal, peaceful party competition? Are there party regimes capable of governing and alternating in power?

MR. SHEEHY: One of the big myths over the last several years is that all of the news out of Africa is bad, focusing too much attention on starvation and chaos. In fact, there has also been a sweeping move toward democracy in Africa. Regimes have come under intense pressure to democratize from the IMF, the World Bank, and Western aid donors, as well as from the very same elites who were enamored for many years with the socialist development model. The fall of the Soviet Union did have a profound effect on the attitude of the elites toward party democracy. It is a very difficult transition for many African countries to make, though.

Kenya, for example, was a very stable country for many years after winning independence but is now being ripped apart by tribalism, as the political parties organize along tribal lines.

Two countries that perhaps are doing the best economically, Ghana and Uganda, are countries led by benevolent dictators. I tend to be sympathetic to the argument that economic liberalization has to come before political liberalization. The governments of Ghana and Uganda have been able to institute some fundamental economic reforms that probably would not have been feasible if they were simultaneously undergoing democratic reforms. This argument holds a great deal of sway with people who are more interested in economics, such as officials in the World Bank, the IMF, and even the U.S. government.

I have worked with the International Republican Institute (IRI). I am familiar with several cases where the IRI has gone into countries to teach people how to form political parties and write political platforms but has encountered resistance from U.S. ambassadors. They argue that reduced subsidies on basic foodstuffs required as the country tries to restructure economically leads to greater social tension and that trying to combine such economic reforms with democratic reform would be too ambitious. Some people argue that economic reform cannot be accomplished without first undertaking political reform. Others argue that the two can be undertaken simultaneously and any arguments to the contrary are just excuses by entrenched elites trying to cling to power. Ultimately, there must be political as well as economic reform if these countries are to be stable. Democracy is an essential component of stability. Aside from South Africa, however, very few countries are developing vibrant, democratic cultures. The military government in Nigeria tried without success to impose a two-party democratic regime on its own terms, and the country remains a strife-torn dictatorship.

QUESTION: I am tremendously interested in your analysis of the trouble spots. Are there any lessons about political fragmentation you have learned in studying Africa that could be applied to the United States? Stepping back from your empirical research, do you see any fundamental principles that should be kept in mind?

MR. SHEEHY: Perhaps the only response I can give is to say that every time I return to Africa, I count my blessings and come away with a real appreciation of how fragile democracy is and how much Americans take our institutions for granted. It is not easy to bring about a democratic culture and develop institutions. Although South Africa was vilified for many years, it did in fact have democratic institutions in place. These institutions certainly did not serve everyone during apartheid, but even the excluded black majority was acclimated to certain democratic political practices. As a result, the transition to democracy was made easier in South Africa. In those African countries where the illiteracy rate is around 80 percent, it is especially difficult to build democratic institutions.

I had a chance to observe voting in rural Kenya. In order to vote, an illiterate would identify himself as such, and the polling agent would then direct that person to a booth and assist him or her in marking the *x* on the ballot. The Kenyan parties did not trust the polling agents, so this procedure would take place under the watchful eyes of 12 party officials, one from each party, making certain that this process was legitimate.

The Clinton administration has dangerously overemphasized democracy as a foundation of our foreign policy because it does not have a good understanding of how difficult the transition to democracy can be. Democracy should be a concern of U.S. foreign policy, but it is no substitute for defending strategic interests.

QUESTION: You argue that the end of the Cold War has reduced U.S. interest in Africa. Meanwhile, a surge of Islamic fundamentalism has occurred in Sudan, Eritrea, Ethiopia, and to some extent, Somalia. I think the United States still has interests there. On a different note, what is the potential of the OAU as a peacemaker and a peacekeeper?

MR. SHEEHY: I do think the OAU is an important organization. Unfortunately, it has been rather ineffectual in addressing conflicts and has no experience with peacekeeping activities.

In case I misrepresented myself, I do *not* think the United States should jump in and intervene in every conflict. I thought the

Somalian endeavor was very dangerous and unwise. In many instances African countries themselves have been loath to get involved in peacekeeping, as the United Nations found out in Rwanda.

The United States still has interests in Africa, but I would argue that they are somewhat diminished now that the Soviet Union is gone. Islamic fundamentalism is a serious challenge to democracy throughout Africa, and there is a particularly deadly struggle being waged today in Algeria.

QUESTION: The national boundaries in Africa were arbitrarily fixed by European colonizers and are thus not in accord with tribal borders, as can be seen in Rwanda and Burundi. Would democratization occur faster if tribes could establish their own countries, so to speak, thereby avoiding struggles among tribes?

MR. SHEEHY: As I mentioned, the OAU is founded on the notion of the inviolability of borders, and talk of territorial changes has traditionally been taboo. Nevertheless, I think it is a question worth asking. Many people would object to redrawing borders, but in some instances it could make a contribution to political stability. For instance, the Hutus and the Tutsis are having a difficult time trying to draw the boundary between them.

Africa already has over 50 states, many of which are inviable. Redrawing borders would probably lead to the creation of more and smaller states. Eritrea seceded from Ethiopia. There are also secessionist movements in Cameroon and Angola. Cabinda is a little speck of land separated from the rest of Angola, but it has the nation's petroleum deposits. Because people in Cabinda do not want to share their oil wealth, they want their own state. It is a real dilemma, and there are no easy answers. I do think it is healthy that people, including Africans, are at least beginning to raise the question of altering borders. Many people saw independence for Eritrea as a real watershed in the debate over the sanctity of state borders.

COMMENT: Couldn't one look at the U.N. experience in the late 1980s as encouraging for future U.N. action? The United Nations did in fact bring to an end a number of regional conflicts—Afghanistan, the Iran-Iraq war, Central America, Libya, and even Cambodia to some extent. These operations were all relatively successful. Perhaps the United Nations did try to do more than its resources allowed, but that was because many new problems came along at the same time, national leaders were distracted by increasing economic problems at home, and there was an increasing reluctance to supply the United Nations with sufficient forces and other facilities to do the job. All of these concerns led to the tendency, particularly on the part of the great powers, to dump a bunch of countries with crucial problems in the lap of the U.N. organization. Politically, it was a way of avoiding involvement.

MR. SHEEHY: I think you make a good point. The United Nations can play a constructive role, as shown in El Salvador, Namibia, and in some other hot spots. Those were classic peace-keeping missions, however. In Namibia, U.N. forces supervised an election, as they did in Cambodia, though they also took on rather sweeping governing powers in the process. The key difference is that a will for peace existed in Namibia and El Salvador. The parties had gotten together and signed a peace agreement. That was not the case in Somalia, Rwanda, and other instances, however. U.N. successes did build a sense of momentum and overconfidence, and the organization took on more than it could handle.

A parallel is often drawn between Namibia and Angola. Some argue that the Angola operation fell apart because of insufficient resources as compared to Namibia. According to this view, the United Nations or the superpowers bear the blame because they were stingy in the case of Angola.

I have studied the Angola issue for several years now, and I can state with a fair amount of confidence that neither UNITA leader Jonas Savimbi nor MPLA leader Dos Santos was willing to accept electoral defeat. That country was going to return to war unless at least one of the parties was willing to concede. My point about Western Sahara is similar. The United Nations can be brought in, but essentially it is just buying time unless the parties are truly ready to make peace. In Namibia there was a unique constellation of forces conducive to peace. South Africa wanted peace, and the Russians and the Americans fell out of the equation. Conditions for peace were not present in Angola. No matter how many resources are allocated to the United Nations, unfortunately, the conflict in Angola will simply have to play itself out before there are hopes of resolution.

COMMENT: You said that the African nations were reluctant to enter into peacekeeping missions. I have been studying this subject a little, and I think that one of the reasons for their reluctance is that they are just not equipped for these missions. If South Africa or the West offered more training and support, perhaps some of the African nations might be more inclined to participate.

MR. SHEEHY: I think you are right. I probably overstated their reluctance. Clearly, the African armies are ill-equipped and do not possess very good logistical capabilities. The United States has been training Ghanaian troops to replace the French troops in Rwanda. It is also providing them with material support–troop carriers, helmets, and so forth. This approach is generally constructive when the mission is fundamentally sound.

There is also a certain political unwillingness among African nations to send troops into peacekeeping operations. No one wanted to go into Rwanda until the United States got involved. Often the United States is a catalyst for increased involvement. No African nations wanted to send troops to Somalia either, but once the United States intervened, some 20 countries became interested. African leaders often have to think how intervention will play domestically. Sometimes it is advantageous for an African regime to send troops; at other times, it is not. They are undoubtedly subject to the same considerations as American presidents are in deciding whether to send troops to a country in conflict.

QUESTION: Isn't there some way to construct a long-range plan in attempting to steer toward some desirable solutions? Is there a U.N. administrative headquarters located in Africa?

MR. SHEEHY: There are some development program offices in Africa, but not military offices.

QUESTION: Why not establish an office somewhere in the central part of Africa to look after African affairs for the United States? Instead of operating out of U.N. headquarters in New York City, why not put some people on the spot to think about solutions to problems in Africa?

MR. SHEEHY: My preference would be to see increased commerce as an important part of the plan. Americans are very generous in promoting overseas development, notwithstanding talk about foreign aid cuts or the lower percent of GNP that the United States government spends on foreign aid compared to Sweden or other industrial countries. In truth, however, foreign aid has not been particularly helpful in Africa. In fact, one can argue that in many ways, foreign aid has led to many of Africa's problems, including some of the famine conditions. The U.S. foreign aid budget for Africa is now slightly more than a billion dollars a year, but American corporations, charity groups, and individuals give $6-7 billion a year in private funds for development activities abroad, with a large portion of those funds going to Africa. There are American groups doing good work in Africa.

President Clinton recently led a conference on African affairs at the White House. The goal in part was to attempt to build a constituency for Africa among Americans, most of whom have no natural inclination toward, or understanding of, Africa. It is a very difficult place in which to travel and has a unique array of problems. Nevertheless, the United States can contribute to positive change in Africa.

NARRATOR: You have introduced a subject to which we should all give more thought. Thank you for sharing your experiences and understanding of Africa with us.

CHAPTER EIGHT

Genocide in Rwanda and the International Response*

ALISON L. DES FORGES

NARRATOR: Alison Des Forges is a graduate of both Yale and Harvard, with her bachelor's degree *magna cum laude* from Harvard and her master's and doctorate degrees from Yale. She is a faculty member of the Department of History at the State University of New York at Buffalo. She chaired the International Commission on Human Right Abuses in Burundi and co-chaired a similar commission on abuses in Rwanda. She is consultant to Human Rights Watch on Africa, focusing both on Rwanda and Burundi. Ms. Des Forges has been a consultant to the U.S. Agency for International Development (USAID) and has testified before subcommittees on Africa for both the Senate and the House. She has also testified and advised members of the National Security Council and the State Department, Ambassador Madeleine Albright, the Canadians, the French, the Belgians, and the European Community. She has also been featured on CNN, "60 Minutes," and "Nightline." She has been featured in articles in the *New Yorker* and has been published in the *New York Times*, the *Washington Post*, and other publications. She is a preeminent figure in the field, and we feel fortunate that she could be with us.

MS. DES FORGES: I often feel that the more I attempt to explain Rwanda, the less I understand. The complexity of the issues, the

**Presented in a Forum at the Miller Center of Public Affairs on 24 February 1995.*

extent of the horror, and the pain and suffering are so monumental that it is difficult for anyone, even someone who has spent 25 years studying the country, to find an explanation for this situation. I would like to discuss the genocide and its implications for U.S. policy and the international tribunal.

A discussion of Rwanda must begin within the context of extraordinary poverty. Many African nations are poor, but Rwanda is one of the poorest. Ninety-five percent of the population still live on their own agricultural subsistence, and a spiraling population growth rate has made less and less land available to sustain that population. Therefore, a situation of extreme economic difficulty existed before the political complications arose.

Understandably, Rwanda had been a sort of cherished child of various foreign aid donors. It is a beautiful, tiny country–only a few hours from border to border by car. It seemed manageable, not like Nigeria or Sudan or Zaire, where the enormity could be overwhelming. In addition, Rwanda has a pleasant climate, so aid providers loved to work there. It has a hard-working population that appears sincerely committed to a work ethic. Hence, to an extraordinary extent, deadlines and quotas were met.

Given these conditions and the fact that its poverty was clearly a pressing problem, Rwanda received a substantial amount of international assistance during the 1970s and 1980s, which did make a difference. In fact, a useful infrastructure was established, including good roads and communications.

The economic success, however, led aid donors to ignore some of the less encouraging signs on the political front. In this ignorance, they were much like the old colonial administration that ignored abuses and outright exploitation as long as taxes were collected, corvée labor was done, and roads, schools, and clinics were built. The colonialists, first the Germans and later the Belgians, supported an elite of chiefs drawn from the Tutsi, who constituted a minority of about 15 percent of the population. As the control of the elite grew more oppressive, the majority ethnic group, the Hutu, organized a revolution that overthrew the elite, including the king, in 1959. In this revolution, the Hutu killed some 20,000 Tutsi and drove hundreds of thousands of others into exile in neighboring countries.

The new republic established by the Hutu discriminated against those of the Tutsi minority left in the country, limiting their access to education and employment. Aid donors willingly overlooked this discrimination so long as the economy seemed to be developing satisfactorily. In 1991, as part of a USAID mission to examine possible projects for promoting democracy in Rwanda, I advised that no further aid be given to the Rwandan government unless it agreed to drop the practice of registering the population by ethnic group. In a holdover from the colonial era, the government required such registration and required all adults to carry identity cards that stated their group affiliation. I concluded that it was contrary to fundamental principles of democracy to support such a practice and that it was in fact counterproductive to provide assistance to a government–supposedly for the purpose of democratization–as long as the government persisted in such categorization. This recommendation was ignored, not just by the U.S. government, but also by other aid-giving governments whose representatives had attended the briefing in which our recommendations were presented. When the genocide began in April 1994, Tutsi were selected for slaughter on the basis of these identity cards.

The generally favorable economic situation took a severe downturn in the mid-1980s, in large part because of a sudden drop in the world price of coffee, Rwanda's primary export. Rwanda, once one of the more promising examples of economic development, became one of many African nations seriously in debt. Because of its previously favorable record, aid donors continued their assistance, but at the same time they imposed a program of economic reform that made life even harder for the ordinary people.

As the economic situation worsened, both aid donors and opposition groups inside Rwanda began to press for political change. The Hutu elite, which had become increasingly repressive and corrupt during its 20 years in power, had lost support even with people of its own ethnic group. With both Tutsi and many Hutu demanding reform, the government led by Juvénal Habyarimana agreed in 1991 to end the single-party system. Opponents of Habyarimana immediately formed a number of new political parties. At about the same time, refugees from the 1959 revolution who had lived for some 30 years in adjacent nations, largely unassimilated and unwanted, decided to insist on their right to return home. They organized the Rwandan Patriotic Front (RPF) and invaded Rwanda on 1 October 1990, intending to assure the refugees of their right to return and, if possible, to overturn the Habyarimana government.

The military officer who commanded the northeastern frontier post where the invasion took place had warned the central government two weeks earlier that an invasion was imminent, but he had not received the reinforcements that he requested to strengthen his detachment. It appears that the Habyarimana government saw the invasion as an opportunity to rebuild its slipping power base, using the attack from the outside to shore up solidarity within the country. Habyarimana and his supporters used the RPF invasion to make scapegoats of the Tutsi within the country and of those Hutu, opposed to Habyarimana, who were willing to tolerate and work with Tutsi. All of these people were lumped into a single category called "accomplices," a fifth column, the traitors, who were said to have supported the invasion.

Within 48 hours, this move led to a series of human rights abuses that first attracted the attention of several international human rights groups, including Human Rights Watch and Amnesty International, and also provoked the formation of some active and useful Rwandan human rights organizations. The government imprisoned about 10,000 people on the charge that they were accomplices and held them without any formal proceedings for months at a time. Many were tortured, and many died in inhumane circumstances.

Even more dramatic, however, the government launched its first massacre of Tutsis within two weeks of that first invasion. I was astonished to hear from the survivors that the killing had been organized by a local government official called a burgomaster. The burgomaster had told people in the commune, the local government unit, that their corvée labor for the month of October 1990 was to kill Tutsis.

Before I became involved in human rights activism, I was primarily a historian who collected oral history. Anyone who works with oral history knows the value of symbolic speech. When I heard the accounts of the massacre, my initial reaction was, "Wait a minute. They don't literally mean that the local government officials said to 'go kill your neighbor.' What they mean is somehow or other, the people in power were involved." Corvée labor was a holdover from the colonial period that had been continued by the independent government as a way to build up the country. Ordinarily it involved work such as repairing the roads and building new schools or health clinics. When I interrogated some of the people accused of the killing, they all admitted to having participated, but they said they had killed those people because the burgomaster had told them it was their corvée for the month.

This pattern, which was so clear in October 1990, was repeated again in January and February 1992, in December 1992 and January 1993, and again in the Great Genocide. From the beginning it was clear that this remarkably successful state was using its administrative network to promote the killing of a part of its population.

When I began lobbying in Washington for decisive American action during the genocide last spring, the refusals I received almost universally began with a reference to Somalia. "We have seen what Somalia is like. We know that Rwanda is also a sinkhole and we do not want to become involved. Our interests are not involved, and it is the sort of situation we can never sort out," they would say. I tried to explain that although Rwanda is on the same continent, it is not another Somalia; it is the opposite. Somalia has no strong tradition of a state structure, and there were indeed competing factions struggling for power. Rwanda, on the other hand, had had 400 years of highly centralized state organization. It was a successful state–not a failed state. In fact, it was too successful in carrying out its targeted policies, which were to kill the minority.

The international human rights community began to protest and to ask for international action during the years of the smaller massacres. In March 1993 we compiled a 160-page report documenting the involvement of the Rwandan government in the killing of its citizens. We submitted the report to the U.N. Human Rights Commission and were told, "Not this year; we already have too many African countries on the docket." We submitted it to the U.S. government, where it did produce some change in policy. For instance, there was a reduction in U.S. government aid, and the remaining aid was taken from governmental channels and funneled through nongovernmental channels.

In Belgium the report had a direct and dramatic result. Within two hours of the publication of the report, Belgium recalled its ambassador. After a flurry of international criticism, the extremists in charge of the Rwandan government, including President Juvénal Habyarimana, changed their strategy but not their goal. They took the power to organize the killing out of the hands of the administrative officials and put it into the hands of the militia, which was attached to the president's political party. They removed the killing one step from the direct authorization of the administrative hierarchy so that it would not be directly traceable to them. In effect, they privatized the violence.

In the earlier massacres, the national radio had played an important role in inciting people to kill, and that tactic also was changed. A private radio station was organized, and the task of inciting violence was placed into the hands of that station.

Events in Burundi also influenced the course of events in Rwanda. Rwanda's demographic twin, Burundi, is located to the south of Rwanda. Its history is quite different because there was no revolution there. There have also been problems, however, between the Hutu and the Tutsi in Burundi. The Hutu majority won a free and fair election in June 1993. It was the first time a Hutu president had ever been elected, and everyone applauded the election vigorously because it set a wonderful example. In October 1993, however, the army, which had remained in the hands of the Tutsi minority, assassinated the president. Approximately 50,000 people died in the weeks of massive violence that followed. There was virtually no reaction in the international community to this atrocity, but there was a reaction next door in Rwanda. In part because of the massive interchange of refugees between these two countries, the events that occur in one country invariably create echoes in the other. Particularly important was the fact that this assassination seemed to indicate to the Hutu in Rwanda that the Tutsi were not to be trusted–that Burundi had witnessed the wonderful election of a Hutu and that the Tutsi had killed him. This incident provided valuable propaganda material for increasing hatred of the Tutsi minority within Rwanda. An even more important consequence of these events stemmed from the failure of the international community to react to the massive slaughter in Burundi. This inaction led the extremists in Rwanda to believe that one could slaughter one's opponents and not be punished, that massacre and even genocide was an acceptable tactic for winning and retaining political power.

Beginning in October 1993, the preparations for killing within Rwanda clearly accelerated. The militia recruited and trained more people, and arms were widely distributed to anyone who was believed to be a supporter of the clique of extremists. This activity was so alarming that in December 1993 the bishop of one of the large Catholic dioceses issued a pastoral letter asking why guns were being distributed in his parishes. Not only were guns being distributed, but grenades as well, which were much more effective and easy to use.

The preparations were clear. The Radio of Hate was broadcasting increasingly virulent calls to violence daily, both against the Tutsis in general and against individuals targeted as members of the government and human rights activists. A colleague and friend, Monique Mujyawamariya, was targeted frequently by this radio station. It would play popular songs with the name *Monique* in the lyrics, and when the song finished, the disc jockey would say something to the effect of, "We have our own Monique here in this country. We all know who she is and what a traitor she is. We all know how she deserves to die. She deserves to be crucified in her front yard and eaten by dogs!" The diplomatic community in Kigali was well aware of the content of these broadcasts and of the preparations for violence, but there was a sense that the international community was almost a victim of its own success.

In August 1993, the war between the guerrilla force–the RPF–and the government in power had finally been settled by the Arusha peace agreement. This peace agreement had come about largely as a result of the active intervention of the international community, particularly the United States and various other actors through the United Nations. Therefore, when preparations for the April 1994 killing campaign increased and the violence finally began, the international community was reluctant to intervene too dramatically, not only because of Somalia, but because the United States and the

United Nations had been successful as mediators in the previous conflict. They were afraid to sacrifice the potential role that they could play by supporting one side or the other. What they failed to consider was that the extremists were willing to use genocide as a strategy of war and that doing so had sufficiently altered the moral and legal climate. Thus, it was no longer a legitimate position for the United States or any other state to abstain from action for the purpose of maintaining neutrality. Neutrality is not possible in the face of genocide, and it was clear within 48 hours that this action would amount to genocide. The press and the human rights organizations reported that this attack was a targeted massacre of the Tutsi people.

I watched little of the genocide on television because it was too awful. I saw one film clip, however, in which people attempting to flee were stopped at a roadside barrier and asked for their identity documents. All of the people with identity papers that were stamped with a "T" (for Tutsi) were taken to the side of the road and slaughtered. These barriers were placed not only on the major roads, but on the footpaths as well. One reason the slaughter was so complete was there was no place to go or flee. The farthest one could go was perhaps to a neighborhood church, hospital, or school, but those places that had in the past been places of refuge became the major areas of killing. We have accounts of astonishing casualty and death rates for thousands of people killed in churches, at the foot of altars, in confessionals, and in the pews. Patients were killed in their hospital beds. These attempts to extirpate a people were absolutely ruthless and systematic. Anyone who was Tutsi or was willing to tolerate or work with the Tutsis was killed. This aggression was so systematic that some of the killers would arrive at a church at 8:00 a.m. and kill people until 4:00 p.m. and then go home, only to return the next day to repeat their murderous activities. This went on day after day until there was no one left. People would sometimes beg to be killed so that they would not have to wait until the next day, but if the killers were tired, the victims were told they would have to wait.

One of the wonders of modern communication was that for quite some time the telephone lines remained open. I had women call me and say, "They came today and killed my husband. They will come back for me tomorrow." There was nothing I could do; the women were killed the next day. It was a systematic effort that was known about from the earliest stages.

We took this information to the U.N. Security Council and to all of the authorities in Washington. I cannot complain about access because I was given access to everyone except the President himself, and the information I have related to you was also communicated to them. The credibility of Human Rights Watch and other organizations involved in this lobbying effort was considerable, and I have no reason to think that my information was doubted. Still, my efforts produced no action. When I asked at the end of each of these meetings what I could do to produce results, I was told in every case to speak to the press and get the information to the public. Clearly, the message was that the government was not feeling the pressure, that there was not enough public demand for action. Given the priorities of the national agenda, genocide in Rwanda was simply not important enough to require action. Additionally, the Rwandan case was the first to be examined under the new presidential directive on peacemaking initiatives.

The United States led the effort to withdraw the U.N. troops in Rwanda. Nearly 3,000 armed soldiers were there at the time the genocide began. Two weeks later, under U.S. leadership, the Security Council voted to withdraw all but 270 soldiers. The Canadian commanding general in charge of those troops told me and others that if he had been given permission to use his troops at any point during those first two weeks, he could have stopped the genocide, but he was not allowed to do so.

There were 10 Belgian peacekeeping soldiers killed the first day. They were killed because they had gone to defend the prime minister, who, although a Hutu, had been willing to work with the Tutsi. The Belgians were killed in part as the result of a deliberate strategy. The people who had planned the attack understood that the Belgians, like the Americans and others, did not want to sacrifice their own soldiers. Ten casualties were too many in the same way that 18 casualties were too many for the United States in Somalia. Therefore, the attackers specifically targeted the ten Belgian soldiers because the Belgian troops were the best-equipped and the best-trained troops available to the U.N. force. They killed them in the most gruesome way possible, knowing that the effect on Belgian public opinion would lead to the withdrawal of their soldiers from Rwanda. That is what happened. The Belgians withdrew, and other members of the United Nations refused to fill the ranks that had been depleted. In fact, the United Nations pulled out all of the troops except for those 270 soldiers.

Two weeks later, the first massive outflow of refugees began—not the Goma refugees that came in midsummer, but the first massive outflow to Tanzania. This situation changed the atmosphere somewhat. Rwanda began to appear on television for the first time when a quarter-million refugees left in a 24-hour period, the largest refugee exodus in the world in such a short time.

The next morning I received a call from the Czech ambassador to the United Nations. The Czech Republic was a member of the Security Council. He told me, in essence, "I have been reading your news releases and reports. I have come to the conclusion that something must be done. You can understand that Rwanda is not a national priority for the Czech Republic, but as a human being I cannot sit here and do nothing." Thus he, in conjunction with the Spanish ambassador and the ambassador from New Zealand, turned the situation around in the Security Council. He asked me to meet the following Monday with the council's 10 nonpermanent members to give them a briefing, which I did. It took three more weeks before the Security Council passed a resolution to redeploy the U.N. troops, in part because the United States, though none of its troops were to participate, insisted on moving slowly and ensuring that all of its criteria were met. Once the resolution was passed on 17 May, I remember congratulating the Czech ambassador and saying it was wonderful news and asking when the troops would be back. I had assumed the troops would return in a week to ten days. He looked at me, smiled, and said: "Three months." I replied that it was not possible to wait; people were dying every day by the thousands and the logistical framework already existed. He maintained that it would definitely take three months.

It then took seven weeks for Pentagon authorities to reach a lease agreement with the United Nations for the 50 armored personnel carriers that were needed to take the troops back to Rwanda. When this incident received publicity in the *New York*

Times, the Pentagon's response was that it was necessary to obtain fair-market value for the spare parts and the maintenance contract. I am certain that under normal circumstances we would all approve of our government being careful about such matters, but in a case where thousands of people are dying every day, it is obvious that someone made a mistake. There should have been a way to reduce this delay with an order from the top. Those armored personnel carriers should have been available within one week instead of seven.

It took six months, from 17 May until November, before the deployment of the second U.N. force was completed. At the same time, U.N. human rights monitors were sent to the country in an operation that, despite the appalling lack of organization, has had some fortunate repercussions. Some wonderful and dedicated people are doing their best to make this program work despite bureaucratic obstacles.

Finally, I would like to mention the consequences of genocide and its implications for Rwanda, Burundi, Zaire, and, in fact, all of mankind. The Genocide Convention, to which the United States is a party along with all of the members of the United Nations, binds each signatory to suppress and prevent genocide. The Security Council resolutions concerning Rwanda used the exact legal language of the Genocide Convention but never used the word *genocide* itself. Moreover, the White House issued a directive in June 1994 instructing American officials to avoid using the word *genocide* when discussing Rwanda with the press, presumably because using the word would increase pressure on the administration to act. Despite these initial refusals to respond, one fortunate reaction to the slaughter of between half a million and a million people was a late surge of interest in punishing the guilty and a realization that a crime of this magnitude simply cannot be ignored without becoming a statement that humankind no longer has any standards to uphold.

An international tribunal has been established, and I am confident it will bring some of the chief perpetrators to account for what they have done. The U.S. government has taken a firm position on this issue and to its credit has been supportive both in terms of personnel and funding for the tribunal. At the same time, there is a desperate need for trials within Rwanda, because the international tribunal will not deal with more than 50 to 100 people. It simply is too cumbersome and too expensive to handle any more than that number. Thus, without trials in Rwanda, there is no way that national reconciliation can occur. Justice must first be done.

The consequences of continued injustice are of great importance in the immediate future for Burundi, where the situation is extremely precarious and where many of the same kinds of preparations for a large-scale slaughter are taking place. I am convinced that unless there is some fairly prompt and effective sanction against the Rwandans who attempted to use genocide as a political tool, the international community will soon find the same situation occurring in Burundi, Zaire, Kenya, and other susceptible places in the world.

NARRATOR: We are all deeply moved by what you have said. You have introduced information that is not fully familiar to many of us. There is an axiom of Roman law that no one is obligated beyond his capacity in any instance, and it seems that this is the crux of the matter when dealing with public policy and foreign policy. Can you address this issue in terms of both obligation and capacity?

MS. DES FORGES: Although I am a novice in the area of public policy, being primarily a historian dealing with the 18th century and having been pulled into the Rwandan situation by the death of many people with whom I had long and close contacts, I did know enough about lobbying Washington not to ask for American troops. Never did we suggest that American soldiers be sent to Rwanda to stop the genocide. All we asked was that the United States cooperate in organizing such a response through the United Nations with African troops. Some African nations were willing to provide these troops, but they needed equipment and logistical support.

How much are we willing to pay to stop a genocide? That question could be debated for a long time. An initial outlay of $10 million in early June would have provided the military equipment and the armored personnel carriers necessary to move troops into the area fairly quickly. The *New York Times* had a wonderful editorial which concluded that the United Nations should try Avis the next time it needed to rent armored personnel carriers.

Instead of the $10 million at the beginning of June, the U.S. government spent approximately 50 times that amount in humanitarian assistance to deal with the refugee crisis that began at the end of July. In terms of pragmatic funding questions, the government should ask at what point and what amounts it should invest in preventive measures to avoid a much larger expenditure later.

Part of the problem is that the government does not receive high marks or much public credit for preventive action because if the disaster does not occur, no one knows what a wonderful thing it did. If the disaster is simply allowed to take place, however, then the government can become a hero by saving two million lives. It seems to me that within the limits of what the United States was asked to provide–50 armored personnel carriers that were sitting in mothballs–the demands were not beyond its means.

Admittedly, the African countries willing to provide the troops hoped to use this opportunity to stock up on fancy equipment and supplies that were not required for this particular confrontation. I also admit that their proposals were a form of blackmail–that they pressured the countries with money because those countries were not willing to provide soldiers. But, if Americans are not willing to send their sons into this type of situation and yet they believe that genocide must be stopped by force if necessary, then the United States has to be willing to pay the bill.

NARRATOR: How was the Organization of African Unity (OAU) involved? In Liberia it was slow to react, but they finally began to move.

MS. DES FORGES: The OAU actually had a peacekeeping force in Rwanda, one that operated successfully for 15 months. It was the first time the OAU had ever done anything of that nature, but it did not receive much publicity. The U.N. troops were deployed after OAU peacekeeping efforts and were not linked to the OAU.

QUESTION: What was the source of the grenades and the weapons that were used to carry out this genocide and what hope is there of some kind of punishment for the instigators?

MS. DES FORGES: Human Rights Watch has a division that deals only with arms trade and its consequences in human rights abuses. It has found that tracking the big weapons is not difficult, but tracking the little weapons is almost impossible. Grenades and AK-47 rifles are produced in so many varieties and forms, in so many factories, and in so many parts of the world that it is almost impossible to track their distribution. The availability of cheap arms in African countries and in other parts of the Third World is a constant problem. Grenades are readily available in markets next to tomatoes for a dollar per grenade. One can imagine the consequences this availability has for the state of law-and-order within a country. The French provided many of the weapons, both directly and by subsidizing a substantial purchase of arms from Egypt. The extremist government in Rwanda mortgaged its tea crop for the next five years to buy guns from Egypt and South Africa, and that arrangement was underwritten by Credit Lyonnais, a bank then partially owned by the state. In addition, arms from numerous sources are still coming into the refugee camps in Zaire. The government responsible for genocide fled across the border and dragooned a substantial portion of the population into accompanying it. Some people fled from fear of the Rwandan Patriotic Front, while others fled because they had been involved in the killings and did not want to be caught. Other people fled simply because the same government that had been giving them orders for years gave them orders to leave.

QUESTION: Who is running the country now?

MS. DES FORGES: The RPF, which was the original guerrilla force that invaded in 1990, defeated the government guilty of genocide and drove it from the country. The RPF is predominantly Tutsi. They established a coalition government with other internal opposition political parties. Lest one believe this is a simple case of good guys and bad guys, let me say that the new government has also been guilty of some serious human rights abuses, including reprisal killings, but certainly not of genocide. This government argues that many of their soldiers are suffering under the enormous emotional impact of arriving home to find their entire families slaughtered, and they react by killing the people who they feel are responsible. That motivation may underlie some of the violence, but it is certainly not the explanation for all of it.

Our present concern is to ensure that the people accused of genocide are brought to trial with due process in an orderly fashion. At this point there are approximately 20,000 accused people who have been jammed into prisons by the new government.[1] One cannot complain too much because it is better that they are imprisoned than shot. At least there is hope that they will be given trials, but in the meantime they are in inhumane conditions.

There are serious problems both in terms of money and human resources in making the judiciary function. The judicial system was never in great shape, but now only 30 of 100 magistrates and perhaps 10 of 70 prosecutors remain. The justice minister is beginning to rebuild, but for a long time he was running his ministry from a hotel room where he also ate and slept. He had no vehicle, telephone, computer, or typewriter–just paper and pencil. This situation has been remedied somewhat. The U.S. Embassy has lent him a vehicle and there have been various international commitments of money to make the judicial system work.

QUESTION: What is the underlying factor involving Kenya?

MS. DES FORGES: Like a number of other heads of state, President Moi in Kenya has made use of the divisions among peoples to solidify his own political power. Recently, Kenya began a policy of requiring people to register and carry identity papers that indicate their ethnic group. This requirement is a negative step that could provide the means for selecting people for killing.

---

[1]Professor Des Forges indicated in early 1997, just before this volume went to press, that the number of detainees had risen to more than 94,000.

QUESTION: I was interested in your comments about the U.N. troops originally stationed in Rwanda and the Canadian officer who said they probably could have stopped the genocide. Could you expand on this subject? How many troops were there?

MS. DES FORGES: There were 2,700 troops. The killing was at first done largely in the capital city of Kigali, although some killing took place in outlying towns as well. In all likelihood, the U.N. troops could not have made much difference in the outlying areas. Given that this state was tightly centralized and that communication was so good from Kigali outward, however, if the U.N. forces had effectively and vigorously brought the situation under control in Kigali, they would have had an impact in outlying regions within 24 hours as well. The situation would have required that U.N. soldiers go into the streets and stop the groups engaged in the killing.

There were two main groups of killers. One was the presidential guard, which was composed of trained soldiers using firearms. Stopping them would have been relatively costly. The other group was the militia, operating sometimes with grenades and at others times with machetes. Those individuals could have been stopped relatively quickly by any professional armed force. In effect, those militia elements have succeeded in terrorizing the international community to such an extent that it is impossible to find any nation in the world that will provide soldiers to challenge them in the refugee camps in Zaire. The visual impact of all of the awful scenes of killing in Rwanda has been implanted in people's minds; thus, when they consider confronting the killers responsible for the deaths of perhaps a million people, they assume they would be confronting an overwhelmingly ruthless and indomitable force.

What many people have forgotten is that the victims had no organization. They were seeking only to hide, and they had no weapons. People did try to resist in some instances. One can see remnants of wooden benches, for example. People ripped the legs off the benches with their bare hands and used them to try to defend themselves. In most cases, however, they had no weapons with which to fight back. The militia obviously mowed them down with no trouble at all. If the militia had been confronting a line of soldiers armed with even riot gear and tear gas, I am convinced they would have retreated.

QUESTION: What happened to the 270 soldiers who remained? Were they in great danger?

MS. DES FORGES: One was killed by accident in the course of a mortar attack between the guerilla force and the old government. A second soldier died also without being deliberately targeted. In addition to the ten Belgian soldiers killed on the first day, these two soldiers were the only U.N. casualties.

QUESTION: Can you describe the role of nongovernmental organizations (NGOs)?

MS. DES FORGES: The extent to which human rights has become a central determinant of policy is extraordinary, even though I wish it could be even more central in some cases. Generally, it is NGO assessments that qualify or disqualify a government in terms of its human rights behavior. This process gives NGOs a power they had not previously anticipated having. It is one thing to stand outside and yell; it is another to be invited in and be heard. Sometimes the NGOs are a little overwhelmed by their own success.

The role of NGOs in policy-making also deserves some consideration because the lines of responsibility are questionable. NGOs like to believe they are honest and conscientious and that they are doing a serious job in collecting information, but perhaps there are some that are not. How can the influence of an extra-governmental operation be built into a policy-making system when the organization is responsible to no one except those who provide financial support?

The other aspect of the NGOs is the enormous importance of all of those humanitarian agencies that actually provide the relief. One of the critical aspects of the situation in the refugee camps in Zaire has been that those agencies which brought in the food could not themselves distribute it. They had to rely on others, and the people on whom they relied were the old authorities guilty of genocide. Thus, NGOs, which are ordinarily perceived as doing an exemplary job, were obliged to support the people guilty of genocide, in effect providing them with control of the food, medicine, and water supplies that are basic to people's lives. By obtaining control over the resources, these old authorities were able to reestablish their hold over the refugee population. Considerable soul-searching has been done among the NGOs over how that situation could have been avoided. The people who made the decisions in central Africa did so to the best of their ability. This fact is another indication of how difficult the problem is to resolve.

NARRATOR: We have discovered today that in addition to your good writings, you are also a moral and intellectual powerhouse. We feel privileged to have heard you and hope we will again have that privilege.

www.ingramcontent.com/pod-product-compliance
Ingram Content Group UK Ltd.
Pitfield, Milton Keynes, MK11 3LW, UK
UKHW021034150926
475561UK00003B/100

9 780761 808510